Winning Women

Stories of Award-Winning Educators

Sandra Harris
Julia Ballenger
Faye Hicks-Townes
Carolyn Carr
Betty Alford

ScarecrowEducation
Lanham, Maryland • Toronto • Oxford
2004

Published in the United States of America
by ScarecrowEducation
An imprint of The Rowman & Littlefield Publishing Group, Inc.
4501 Forbes Boulevard, Suite 200, Lanham, Maryland 20706
www.scarecroweducation.com

PO Box 317
Oxford
OX2 9RU, UK

British Library Cataloguing in Publication Information Available

Library of Congress Cataloging-in-Publication Data

Winning women : stories of award-winning educators / Sandra Harris . . . [et al.].
    p. cm.
  Includes bibliographical references.
  ISBN 1-57886-158-6 (pbk. : alk. paper)
  1. Women school administrators—United States. 2. Women educators—United
States. 3. Educational leadership—United States. I. Harris, Sandra, 1946–
LB2831.82.W56 2004
371.2'011'082—dc22

                                    2004006769

⊗™ The paper used in this publication meets the minimum requirements of
American National Standard for Information Sciences—Permanence of Paper
for Printed Library Materials, ANSI/NISO Z39.48-1992.
Manufactured in the United States of America.

To the women in our lives who encouraged and inspired us and
whose efforts created an environment that enabled us to become leaders;
and to the women who follow us,
many as yet unnamed, who are in the process of becoming. . . .

Those who came before created. . . . Those who follow . . . lead.

The authors donate all proceeds from the sale of this book to
the Sandra Lowery Educational Leadership Scholarship,
Stephen F. Austin State University, Nacogdoches, Texas

Contents

1

Traditional Conflict: Woman or Leader?

Sandra Harris

The suspected witch was submerged in a pond. If she drowned, she deserved to; if she didn't she was a witch. In the first case, God was revealing her nature; in the second, the devil.

—Friedrich von Spee, *Cautio Criminalis*

The traditional public perception of being a woman and being a leader has long been in conflict. Historically, it seems that a woman can not be both—if she is a "true" woman, she cannot be a leader, and if she is a leader, she cannot fulfill her duties as a woman. Indeed, for centuries women's place in life has centered around family and men as nurturer, caretaker, and helpmate (Gilligan, 1993). Examples of women's leadership roles were often dismissed, or kept quiet at best, a dilemma reflected in classical literature. Just consider the following:

- Shakespeare (1564–1616): "Such duty as the subject owes the prince, Even such a woman oweth to her husband." (*The Taming of the Shrew*, Act IV, Sc. 1, line 142)
- George Herbert (1593–1632): "Words are women, deeds are men." (*Jacula Prudentum*)
- Alexander Pope (1688–1744): "She who ne'er answers till a husband cools, Or if she rules him, never shows she rules." (*Moral Essays*, Epistle II, line 261)

WOMEN IN THE WORKFORCE

Until the early 1800s, most married couples in the United States worked together in farming or small household businesses. At about this time, a wage-labor system supplanted widespread self-employment, and workers began working away from the farm and the home. When this occurred, typically, men worked in these jobs, and household work and child care became solely the domain of the wives. While poor women continued to work outside the home, other groups were likely to quit paid work after marriage (Coontz, 2000).

During the 1920s, an increasing number of office jobs in a much more urban economy drew many women into the workforce. During the 1930s and the 1940s, women of all but the wealthiest families once again began to work outside the home. After 1970, the fastest growing group of female workers were mothers of young children, and by the 1990s, over 55% of working mothers went back to work before their child was even a year old (U.S. Census Bureau, 1998). Today, most marriages, even with children, have a husband and a wife who work outside the home.

BACKGROUND OF WOMEN'S ROLE IN EDUCATION

Thomas Jefferson, who proposed the first plans for public schooling in the U.S., reflected the philosophy of his time when he wrote that women belonged in the home and had little need for education except as "might enable them, when they become mothers, to educate their own daughters, and even to direct the course for sons, should their fathers be lost, or incapable, or inattentive" (as cited in Tozer, Violas, & Senese, 1998, p. 39). Jefferson went on to add that education for women should emphasize dancing, drawing, and music. Yet women did become educated; and today, over 56.5 million women are in the workforce. Consequently, in most cases, the decision of whether women should work outside the home has become a personal family decision rather than one limited by societal perception. Yet, the struggle for women to be recognized as leaders in the workplace, specifically in education as teacher, central office administrator, principal, or superintendent, still continues.

Leadership in Classroom Teaching

Even though today 70% of teachers are women (Steffy, 2002), many women choose to teach because they feel career options are limited. Despite the prevalence of women in teaching, of even greater concern is that men continue to dominate in educational leadership roles. In 1857, the National Education Association (NEA) offered membership to male teachers. Women were eligible for honorary membership only and were not allowed to speak from the platform; if they wanted ideas or papers shared, they had to find a male member to do the presentation. By 1866, women were allowed full membership in NEA. However, soon a conflict arose among the established male leadership and classroom teachers, led by women, that centered around the "leadership's neglect of classroom teachers' welfare and [their] preoccupation . . . with controlling the membership and offices of the most influential units" (Ortiz & Marshall, 1988, p. 124). It was not until 1904 that Margaret Haley, leader of the Chicago Teachers' Federation, delivered the first major address by a classroom teacher from the NEA convention platform; it was titled "Why Should Teachers Organize?"

In 1910, Ella Flagg Young became the first woman elected to the presidency of NEA, although one male member commented that this was "the one regrettable feature of the meeting" (as cited in Ortiz & Marshall, 1988, p. 124). Eventually, there was a tacit agreement that the presidency would be rotated every other year between males and females, which is still observed by NEA.

Most recently, site-based decision making has been adopted by many states across the nation. This is a leadership policy based on the premise that those closest to the source (teachers to students) should be involved in making decisions at all levels of the school. Consequently, classroom teachers today serve on committees for hiring, budgeting, designing curriculum, adopting discipline policies, and long-range planning, resulting in greater participation in leadership activities.

Leadership in Administration

The superintendency has historically been conceived of in "distinctly male terms" (Grogan, 2000, p. 121). For example, the Committee of Ten of 1892 that formulated policies for superintendents included only men. Other early leaders recommended that education adopt a business model and hire administrators from these ranks, which, of course, excluded women. At the turn of the 20th century, the business influence on American schools became even greater. For example, from 1865 to 1910 the superintendent had been seen as a scholar-educator and a teacher of teachers, but in later years he became more of a "business manager–school executive type" (Ortiz & Marshall, 1988, p. 125). Glass (1992) refers to the superintendency as the "most male-dominated executive position of any profession in the United States" (p. 8), and, until recently, even the language used to describe the superintendent has been almost completely male: *statesman*, *he*, *warrior* (Grogan, 2000). Even today, when over half of students enrolled in educational administration classes are women, only 13% of all superintendent positions are held by women (Glass, Bjork, & Brunner, 2000).

Interestingly, female mid-level administrators actually constituted 55% of elementary principals in 1928, 41% in 1948, 38% in 1958, 22.4% in 1968, and 19.6% in 1973 (Johnson, 1973). However, in the1980s, 25% of principals were women, and by the early 1990s this had risen to 48%. Most were elementary principals, with only 12% serving at the high school level (Natale, 1992; Saks, 1992). Central office positions have typically been the most likely administrative level at which women are represented, with as many as 48.2% of women filling general administration positions, such as finance or personnel (Ortiz & Marshall, 1988).

BARRIERS TO LEADERSHIP

In 1909, Ella Flagg Young envisioned that "women are destined to rule the schools of every city . . . she is no longer satisfied to do the greatest part of the work and yet be denied leadership" (Blount, 1998, p. 1). While certainly there are many more opportunities for women in leadership today, Young's prediction has fallen far short of its target in schools. Yet this conflict for leadership is not isolated in education alone but continues to dominate other careers for women as well. Consider the following:

- Between 1970 and 1980 the increase in women holding managerial and administrative positions in the U.S. workforce increased by nearly 100% (Bass, 1990). Yet, women remain underrepresented in business leadership positions (Banks & Banks, 1995).

- Women hold only 13% of management-level jobs and 7% of top-level positions (Holtkamp, 2002).
- Women make up 27% of lawyers, but only 13% earn partnerships. In banking, 67% are women, yet only 13% are top executives (Allison, 2000).
- In higher education, women make up 43% of tenure track professors, but only 26% have tenure (Orenstein, 2000).
- Women earn only 75 cents for every dollar earned by men (Costello & Stone, 1994).
- Among all *Fortune 500* companies, 393 have no women among their top five executives (Jones, 2003).

What are some of the barriers in this "woman or leader" conflict that continue to plague women educators who choose to become leaders? Often these barriers fall into two primary categories: (1) marriage and family responsibilities and (2) cultural stereotyping.

Marriage and Family Responsibilities

Women who have family responsibilities must consider several factors when making career advancement decisions, all of which focus on the effect their work will have on their families. Thus, when women plan careers, they factor inequality into their futures by assuming they will move in and out of the workforce due to family responsibilities (Orenstein, 2000), a phenomenon called *sequencing* (Jamieson, 1995). In fact, 7 out of 10 women surveyed indicated that they expected their spouses' jobs to take priority over theirs. Thus, even before they begin their careers, most young women decide that their careers will be secondary to their husbands'. While some believe that education, family, and work can occur harmoniously in one's lifetime, others believe that sequencing is harmful to careers because women ultimately have less professional experience than men of the same age.

Prior to 1978, sequencing was often forced on many women, particularly in education. For example, an NEA study in 1930–1931 found that 77% of districts surveyed would not hire married women and 63% dismissed female

teachers if they got married. As recently as 1974, the courts were considering school policies that required pregnant teachers to leave the classroom as
early as the fourth month of pregnancy "to spare children the sight of pregnant women" (Jamieson, 1995, p. 66). It is not unusual for prospective female administrators to be advised by other women to "make sure your children are out of elementary school" before applying for top-level positions
(Lowery & Harris, 2001, p.171).

Traditionally, lack of mobility or being place-bound has been another
barrier to career advancement, limiting many women to only those opportunities in the same area where their families live (Harris, Arnold,
Lowery, & Marshall, 2001; Ramsey, 1997). In fact, Ezrati (1983) found
that 90% of women would not even consider relocating unless their husbands found jobs, yet 75% of men would relocate if they found a better
job regardless of whether or not their spouses found employment. Like-
wise, Thomas Cooke refers to the "trailing wife" syndrome and asserts
that "even when wives have higher-status jobs, the direction of migration
is to help the husbands" (Smith, 2000, p. 1H).

The influence of marriage and family responsibilities on a woman's
work life extends to other areas as well. For example, Ramsey (1997) suggests that a husband's support may exert such a powerful effect on a
woman who becomes superintendent that it can influence her level of success in that role. Also, other studies have indicated that career advancement often causes women to limit family size (Hensel, 1991).

Cultural Stereotyping

An especially important barrier is the traditional stereotyping of leadership, which has failed to address the female perspective and its related
qualities (Irby, Brown, & Trautman, 1999). After all, most of what is
learned in administrative leadership courses comes from male-based experiences. This view is supported by Hudson and Rea's 1998 study, which
showed that while female and male teachers identify the same qualities as
desirable in a principal regardless of the principal's gender, male principals are viewed by females as having legitimate authority based solely on
the position, whereas both males and females say that women must work
to earn their authority. Yet, Colwill (1997) found that while women are

less able than men to influence others, they are more effective at getting things done.

A barrier related to ingrained cultural perceptions of leadership is that of sponsorship or networking. Historically, men have been encouraged toward management and women toward instruction. For years, male organizational leaders have supported and mentored each other in "a good ol' boy" network, filling administrative positions with friends and protégés while largely ignoring qualified women for these positions (Ortiz & Marshall, 1988). Over 30 years ago, Barnett (1971) found that men tended to select careers based on interests, aptitudes, and financial possibilities; women, on the other hand, tended to be influenced in career decisions by career role models or significant others. For example, daughters of working mothers tend to have a higher career orientation than daughters of mothers who do not work outside the home. At the same time, the lack of women mentors or role models in some career fields contributes to the high number of women who still choose traditionally female occupations, such as teaching or nursing.

Additionally, cultural stereotyping has placed women in nonleadership roles, thereby limiting women's goal orientation. While men typically enter education with the goal of becoming a principal or superintendent, women enter teaching with only one goal—becoming a teacher, not becoming a leader in the classroom or in administration (Ortiz, 1982; Pankake, 1995). This same lack of goal orientation often results in women spending more years in the classroom than men. In fact, men often enter administration as early as their mid-20s, while women often wait until their late 40s (Glass, 1992; Shakeshaft, 1989; Zemlicka, 2001).

Clearly, the traditional public perceptions of femininity and of a woman's ability to be an effective leader are often in conflict. Consequently, for women to be seen as leaders in their fields, women must have more credentials than male counterparts, be better prepared, and be more knowledgeable (Jamieson, 1995). Women leaders who adopt seemingly male behaviors, such as assertiveness, often find that while assertiveness is a valued male characteristic, it is not valued in women (Morgan, 1993). Other concerns for "getting the job done" include a fear that women might not be able to be good disciplinarians, construct a budget, or make tough decisions. In fact, when a woman is unsuccessful as an administrator, the school board is unlikely to hire another woman, as though it was her gender that contributed to the failure (Lowery & Harris, 2001).

To overcome these barriers, women must constantly try to balance marriage and family responsibilities and at the same time acknowledge the cultural stereotypes that often provide the framework in which they work. This problem is exacerbated for minority women who face an even greater problem in achieving leadership roles. While they must struggle through these same barriers of family responsibilities and cultural expectations of gender, they are faced with the additional barrier of racism.

BUILDING A BRIDGE TO WOMEN LEADERS

The authors of this book have experienced the conflict of being "woman or leader," yet we believe passionately that it does not have to be that way. Each of us in our own way sought opportunities to build a bridge from the barriers we encountered in our personal and professional lives to become "women leaders." We remember as young school girls in the 1950s and 1960s being asked by adults what we wanted to be when we grew up; before we could answer, the questioner invariably suggested, "A nurse or a teacher?" Of course, we said, "Teacher." None of us expected to become principals, superintendents, or university professors, and so we spent the requisite 10 years in the classroom before moving into administration. We limited the size of our families because we were dedicated to being educators. We were advised to wait until our children were older before accepting more leadership responsibility, and we even gave that advice to others. We were place-bound due to our families. Our career goals were often subverted. As one of our friends commented, "Oh, yes, I've had a well-planned career. I always managed to get a job teaching wherever my husband's career took him."

While one of us was superintendent of a school, we read a year-end evaluation from a teacher that the school "should have a male superintendent." We worked longer hours than our male counterparts, and we saw jobs we were interested in offered to males with less experience. We found it difficult to network and had few mentors or sponsors in positions of importance. After working hard at school all day, we went home to husbands and children, cooked dinner, and still found time to listen to their needs.

Our purpose in writing this book is not to engage in "male bashing." It is not to prove that women make better administrators than men do. Indeed, over the years, we have worked with excellent male educators who often encouraged us and even promoted us. However, we acknowledge that there are differences in women and men. For example, men are more likely to be oriented toward rights, while women are more likely to be oriented toward caring (Gilligan, 1977). According to Ortiz and Marshall (1988), research on women administrators suggests that women leaders focus more closely than men on instructional tasks, as well as on students' individual differences. Relatedly, studies of superintendents note that men exert leadership within and without the organization, while women exert their leadership within the organization and in those activities most closely associated with their role. Other studies reveal that male groups compete with each other and rarely express feelings; male groups are more likely to have a differentiated division of labor; female groups are more often characterized by interpersonal relations and concern for one another; and in mixed groups, men develop a more personal orientation and are less aggressive. Just how valid can educational leadership theory be without considering the experiences of both men and women?

Where were the stories of other women's experiences? Largely for us they were silent. After all, in the past most of the knowledge base for educational leadership did not include the experiences of women. Yet stories and personal experiences offer a powerful opportunity to reflect on the limitations of stereotyping in gender or race or on other societal expectations (Ah Nee-Benham & Cooper, 1998). Stories promote an understanding of women's issues, from family concerns to gender and racial identity, and reveal strategies that individuals use to negotiate barriers and opportunities in their lives (Bloom & Munro, 1995). This is why it is so important for women to "tell their stories and empower other women" (Steffy, 2002, p. 4).

In the following chapters, we tell the stories of nine women leaders who have earned recognition for their contribution to education as teachers, principals, superintendents, and university professors. We deliberately selected women at various levels of education because we believe that leadership occurs at every level. Through extended conversations with these women, their stories enrich our leadership paradigm to include "how personal values, political pressures, and organizational concerns are translated

2

A Warrior for Children

Dawn Lynette Smith by Carolyn Carr

Leadership is about building a community where the children feel
safe, cared for, and loved.

—Dawn Lynette Smith

Dawn Lynette Smith, a diminutive member of the Klamath Tribe, stood
disbelievingly on a balcony overlooking Washington, DC, feeling inspired, honored, privileged, and so unworthy of the award she had just received. She is one of the principals, representing the 50 states, receiving
the 2002 National Distinguished Principal Award. She has just completed
a week in Washington attending amazing and inspiring dinners and re-
ceptions.

Dawn had not expected to be honored in such a way when a teacher in
her small elementary school on the Warm Springs Indian Reservation
heard about the award and wrote a one-page nomination letter to the Oregon Elementary Principals Association. To Dawn's surprise she was
named the Central Oregon Regional Distinguished Principal. Then many
more forms were completed for the Confederation of Oregon School Administrators, and she became the distinguished principal representing Oregon. She invited her nominating teacher to be her guest for the trip, and
they both spent precious dollars on gowns to wear to the reception. Now,
here they both are at the closing ceremony, eating little desserts made to
appear like miniature White Houses. Then the event comes to a close,
with everyone on the balcony, enormously touched and slightly tearful,

ringing the school bells they have been given to honor all the children taught by all the teachers of the nation.

THE STORY BEGINS

The Warm Springs Indian Reservation is in a remote area of central Oregon spread across high desert hills and deep river valleys. Driving down from a high plateau where few signs of habitation are in evidence, a visitor sees the small Warm Springs community located just off the highway. In Warm Springs, buildings still stand that are remnants of the old government Bureau of Indian Affairs boarding school, where the grandparents of the children in school today had their braids cut and native languages banned. Approximately 3,900 residents live on the reservation today. The K–4 elementary school is in the center of the village. A class of small students led by their teachers is crossing the road to the school from a small house across the street. The house substitutes for classrooms and a gymnasium that recently burned.

Upon entering the school, visitors soon learn that the principal, Dawn Smith, does not have an office in the traditional sense. The secretaries explain that she has an office in her old 1st-grade classroom down the hall. The school hallway looks clean and inviting as one walks toward the indicated classroom, which is obviously a working space. Dawn shares it with several other persons, including her assistant principal and a reading specialist. Around the room are banks of computers, stacks of hula hoops, and a horseshoe table at which three kindergartners sit with Dawn, reading. Clearly, Dawn is a unique principal, and her story is an amazing and inspirational one.

Dawn knew from the beginning that she wanted to be a teacher. Her earliest school memory is of walking down the school hallway holding a book, the title of which she still remembers: *The Little Red Hen*. She remembers loving how the book felt in her hands as she touched it and looked at the bright pictures. Her love of books came naturally from both her parents. Her father was a Native American, the first member of the Klamath Tribe to graduate from college. He became a high school teacher and coach, a civil rights activist, and tribal chairman. Perhaps Dawn's biggest influence, her father asserts that Native American families have always seen education as crucial to learning survival skills, even as these skills have evolved and changed over time. Dawn's mother is white and spent her career as a librarian. Dawn speaks of her as the most compassionate person she has ever known.

As a junior high student growing up in Salem, Oregon, Dawn became interested in the State School for the Deaf and volunteered there. She was fascinated by how much difference she made with the students. Consequently, she went to the University of Northern Colorado in Greeley to study deaf education. In her senior year she was unexpectedly contacted by the tribal elders of the Warm Springs Indian Reservation. They were recruiting persons to come to the reservation as teachers. Excited by the opportunity, Dawn accepted the call and transferred to Oregon State University in Corvallis, which was partnering with the reservation. Over the next 4 years, approximately 40 students joined the program and were trained at OSU. Most later became outstanding national educators and tribal leaders. Dawn wanted to fill the education role better than she had experienced it as a child and better than was being done at the reservation at the time. Working toward this goal, she stayed on the reservation as an educator for the next 30 years.

LEADERSHIP STYLE EMERGES

Dawn doesn't know how to describe her leadership style, except as being a member of the collegial community in her building. She remembers being a very directive leader at the beginning of her career as a principal. She had a goal and a vision of helping the students achieve all they could, and she wanted the teachers in the school to catch that vision, to do better and make the school better, to be "warrior teachers" who would fight for the kids. One of the leadership skills she is most proud of is her ability to hire really good teachers who are accountable, teachers who feel a passion for teaching. She tells the story of her ruthlessness in hiring interviews when she first became a principal. She wanted only teachers who would commit to staying at least 5 years, and certainly not those who came in with a "mission" to work with the Native American students, or those who "relate to Native American spirituality." Those attitudes make Dawn shudder as she exclaims, "Give me a break!" Her philosophy is to build the need for accountability as you build the culture of a school.

Today Dawn sees her role as the researcher for resources, finding effective programs, such as effective reading programs, so the teachers can spend their time planning and teaching. She leads the faculty in growing accountability for utilizing best practices, doing the work themselves, not depending on outside experts. Dawn speaks of "the team" all the time. She speaks glowingly about her assistant principal and her teachers as extraordinary educators who are able to do almost anything. She doesn't do it—they do! But she does make it possible for great things to happen, such as the 5-year $300,000 annual grant that the school received to help focus on reading. With the resulting resources, reading scores have gone up every year. Dawn feels she must know about everything that goes on in the school—not just bits and pieces. If teachers are putting data into the computers, she needs to put data into the computer as well in order to help them do their best with that information in the classroom.

EARLY CAREER EXPERIENCES

Ten years into Dawn's career at Warm Springs Elementary School, a new female principal arrived, a most inspirational person who became Dawn's mentor. This woman's vision for the school was to make a positive difference in the lives of the students. Dawn taught 1st grade, but the principal urged her to work toward a counselor's license because of her skill in relating to the children and their parents. Dawn took this advice, commuting 3 hours back and forth for her classes at Portland State University (PSU). She then spent 5 years as a counselor, which she dearly loved because of the opportunity it gave her to teach in every classroom about issues such as mutual respect and self-esteem, topics greatly needed on the reservation.

Dawn speaks with great sorrow about the problems of the "res." The children deal with enormous grief because they see death so frequently. It has been reported (Walth, Christensen, & Sullivan, 2003) that residents on the reservation are three times as likely to die between the ages of 22 and 44 as the statewide average in Oregon. Children die on this reservation at a rate more than three times that of the rest of Oregon, and nearly twice that of Native American children in the northwest and around the country, mostly from accidents, neglect, or violence. Tribal members and others working with the children on the reservation say many opportunities to save lives are lost because laws go unenforced by the tribal council or effective programs are cut back for budgetary reasons. The children cannot escape the ongoing grief. Children on the reservation are also likely to live in poverty. Many have lost family members and are being raised by grandparents or other relatives. Dawn says, "Death is everywhere, and the children are forced to deal with it." Yet a cultural reluctance to speak of death makes it hard to address the children's trauma.

After her first mentor left, Dawn remembers a time of serious decline in the school. Two principals came and left in 4 years. Nearly a third of the teachers left each year. Student behavior spiraled downward; graffiti and vandalism of the school were common. Seventy percent of the students were achieving below grade level. Substitutes avoided working at the school. General chaos reigned. The community wanted Dawn to take over the school, so she applied for the principal position. But the school board refused to give it to her. Instead, they appointed her as the first and only assistant principal in the history of the school. Not to be deterred, she spent the next 2 years learning everything she could about running the school and working with the community. Finally her day came, and she became principal of Warm Springs Elementary School. Almost overnight the school began to change for the better. But another obstacle was soon in her path.

In Dawn's second year as principal she developed excruciating headaches. She was diagnosed with a brain tumor. She told almost no one about what was happening, except her husband and her two children. After surgery for what turned out to be a benign tumor, she lost much of her memory and ability to spell or associate words. Medication caused bizarre hallucinations, and she gained 80 pounds. Undaunted, gradually she worked her way back to a normal life. She became a runner and lost the weight she had gained. Eventually she recovered fully, but she never stopped working for the school. Every waking moment was now devoted to the children and making the school better. Dawn knew she was making a difference, and that awareness propelled her recovery. Yet even with this amazing story, she does not see herself as special. When asked to name three words that characterize her, Dawn can think of none. Her modesty and humility reflect much about her quiet power.

THE POLITICS OF CULTURE AND LEADERSHIP

Dawn sees herself as continually learning and developing her leadership skills. An example of the challenges she has faced relates to the languages and culture of the reservation. Wasco, Warm Springs, and Paiute languages are spoken there. These ancient tribal languages are being lost as elders die and younger generations no longer learn them. Some years ago she worked with the Tribal Culture and Heritage Program to set up a "language school within the school." She set aside time during the day for a few tribal elders to come into the school and deliver instruction to the students in the Sahaptin, Wasco, and Paiute languages and traditions. The goal was to create a symbolic bridge between the past and future of the community by preserving the native languages. There were initial successes, but after 8 years, Dawn realized it wasn't working. Inappropriate things were happening in the classroom; inappropriate things were being said and done to the students in the classes. This was not entirely unexpected because the elders did not have teaching skills and often became impatient with the students.

Dawn debated at length about what to do. Should she just cancel the whole thing, tell the elders to leave the school, and thereby stir up the entire community? She happened to be taking a course at PSU to renew her administrative license. As good fortune would have it, the course was on conflict resolution, and the graduate students had been asked to share a conflict with the class. As Dawn tells the story, her fellow students saved her by advising her to informally explain what was happening to the tribal leaders first and then to people in the community. They told her to share *why* she needed to do what she was planning, instead of just canceling the program outright. She did just that, talking to tribal leaders, parents, and community members, telling them her concerns and what needed to happen for the good of the students. Then she spoke with the school board, and the elders were called in for a meeting. Only when she had the community behind her did she present her formal case, and at that point, both the school board and the elders accepted her judgment without question. She could not have accomplished what she did without causing all kinds of political problems in the community if she had jumped in and done what she had intended at first to do. Typically, she credits her classmates for her success.

LEAVING NO CHILD BEHIND

Discipline is another area where Dawn has made a significant contribution to her school. She recalls an incident when a disgruntled bus driver called the school office insisting on a meeting with the principal about student behavior on his bus. To show the driver respect, Dawn walked out to the street to meet the bus when the driver reached the school. He angrily indicated that he did not want to talk to a mere female teacher; he wanted to see the principal! He obviously expected a male with authority. When she introduced herself as the principal, Dawn recalls that he became very contrite. Despite her small size and gender, her eagle-eyed stare and quiet voice convinced him she could "sweet talk" any misbehaving student out of that bus and deal effectively with the problem.

During her tenure at the school, student behavior has markedly improved. Dawn speaks at length about the respect the community and the students feel for the school today. Before she came, painted graffiti was a common problem, but no longer. She tells about a single incident that occurred a year ago when someone wrote graffiti on the building walls, but did so with *chalk*. It could be washed away easily with water! Such is the respect and love for the school.

Student achievement has steadily improved under Dawn's leadership, but this past year the school failed to make "adequate yearly progress" according to the No Child Left Behind law. Many of the parents were very upset when they didn't make this annual goal. The problem was not because of achievement scores, although the scores went down somewhat because of required disaggregation of scores by subgroups. The scores were still higher than the previous year, as they had been each year, and significantly higher than the 40th percentile scores when she became principal years before. Scores are now into the 70th percentile. The school had not made its goal this year because it had to reach 95% attendance and had only achieved 94.5%. What to do?

Dawn decided not to keep this information quiet, but to let everyone know and enlist community support. She put a notice on the village billboard that they had not met their goal. The notice read that reading scores were up. Math scores were up. All academic goals had been met. The reason the school had failed was attendance. Immediately, upset parents came into the school asking what they could do to help. Now attendance is higher than the required 95%. The parents respond to what she says because they respect the school and everyone there. They know the school faculty cares deeply for the children and that the parents can make a real difference in some ways, and so they do. A large part of parent willingness to help comes from their observation of this principal's personal dedication.

Dawn returns this vote of confidence. Always upbeat, she sees hope in the school, which, under her guidance and leadership, has become an oasis of safety for the children. She is certain that the children coming to school today do not have quite the depth of pain and heavy cycle of grief that were common years ago when she first came to the school and worked with their parents when they were children. She knows that the parents are making a difference because of what they themselves learned in the school. She sees things changing with this generation of children. They are happier; they smile; they walk down the school's hallway reading books!

THE GUIDING PRINCIPAL

Dawn lives near the school, on a hill overlooking the whole valley. She is up at 4:30 A.M. and spends time until 6:30 getting ready for the day by meditating and reading. Then she goes to school and serves breakfast to the kids that arrive on the first bus. She also cleans the tables before she meets the next buses. From 8:00 to 8:30 everyone reads. Then she works in her office on paperwork, visits the classes, and finally is off to the cafeteria to help serve lunch and clean up afterward. She also serves as the school's special education teacher and school counselor. She does all these extra duties as trade-offs because of serious budget cuts. By doing so, she is able to keep her assistant principal, preparing him to replace her when she retires.

At 12:45 she works with three 2nd graders, helping them with reading. From 2:15 to 2:30 P.M., she sits with a 4th-grade boy in a wheelchair who has no vision or movement, cautioning those around him that any sharp noise or movement could bring on a seizure. Her quiet calm and soothing tone seem to please the boy each day during their short interchange. At 3:10 the buses begin to come. She meets them and sees that all the children get home safely.

On the day of my interview with Dawn, a student walked into the space where we were talking and said quietly to Dawn that someone had been sick in the bathroom. Ever so gently, Dawn carefully explained to the student that even though she doesn't usually do so, today she wants the girl to do something different. She acknowledged that she would normally go and clean up the mess, but today she asks the student to please go to the office and tell the secretary to get a custodian to clean up—only this one time, because she has company.

PERSONAL AND PROFESSIONAL BARRIERS

During an especially stressful time in her work Dawn consulted a dear friend, an elderly woman who was one of the tribal chiefs and who had been a mentor for her. This woman had helped Dawn maneuver through the political quagmires of the language school issue and advised her to follow her own initial instincts and not the political patterns of the village. This elder told Dawn that she should start every day by going outside first thing in the morning, before light came, and looking up at the stars. Dawn followed this advice and looked at the stars every morning. Admitting that she did not really see herself as a very spiritual person, she continued this habit of looking at the stars. She didn't really know what the purpose was but would talk about "helping me through the day," "doing the best thing," "making a difference," and other such prayerful statements. Some time afterward she had occasion to tell the elder that she had been doing what she had advised—going out every day, looking up at the stars, and asking for help getting through the day. The elder reacted strongly, "Oh no, Dawn! That's not why I told you to do that. I wanted you to look up and give thanks for the day you have to make a difference in lives; it's to give thanks, not to ask for anything!" Dawn had learned another lesson of humility from her mentor.

Dawn speaks about "being brown" and not knowing at times whether she has faced barriers because of her gender or her skin color. She knows that very few people understand her reaction when she hears people say, "I understand what you mean" or "I know what you mean." She believes no one can understand unless it has happened to them. Often she doesn't know if the discrimination is because she is a woman or because she is brown. But she feels it nevertheless. When a middle school principalship in Warm Springs became available in a previous year, she applied. The challenge of working at a different level was very appealing, even if a bit frightening. To her surprise, she did not get the position; she was told by a tribal leader that the school board would probably never hire a secondary female administrator, implying that a woman could not do the job. She was very angry at first because she knew she *could* do the job. When she was honest with herself she realized she actually did not want to go to the middle school; rather, she wanted the job because she knew she could do it well and make a big difference in the school.

THE IMPACT OF A LIFE

Because of Dawn's leadership, the reservation school has steadily improved the academic achievement of its students, the involvement of parents, and the lives of its children. She has brought grants of several million dollars to the school and used these with enormous effectiveness. But one story captures the real worth of this exceptional woman. It was reported in a feature article in the Portland newspaper the *Oregonian* (Sullivan, 2003) after Dawn won the National Distinguished Principal Award.

One day a 4th-grade girl lost a tooth at lunch, and to her utter dismay, accidentally tossed the tooth into the trash with the remains of her lunch. She reported the disaster to her principal, who immediately plunged into the garbage to find it for the distressed child. After considerable rummaging through the mash of macaroni and green beans, Dawn retrieved the lost molar. She kept it with her as she went outside to supervise the children at play, but as luck would have it, she accidentally dropped the tooth outside. She soon found it again and delivered it safely to the delighted child. The child then took the tooth to the bathroom to clean it, where, unfortunately, it went swirling down the sink drain. But Dawn had taught a lesson that remained in this little girl's heart.

At the formal school celebration at the end of the year for the departing 4th-graders, each child handed a carnation of appreciation to the one person who had made the most difference for them in school. This same little girl shyly handed her carnation to Mrs. Smith, explaining, "She cares about the kids that go to this school."

For Dawn Smith it is all about love, not about achievement or doing something that is better than anyone else. It is about building a community where the children feel safe, cared for, and loved. That is what being a leader is about for her and for the children she has guided for the past 30 years. She is truly a warrior for her school and her people.

Dawn Smith is dedicated to nurturing a learning community in which all children can grow and feel safe. For over 30 years she has worked with steel resolve toward her vision of helping her students achieve all they can. And the work continues today as a new generation of Native American children comes to school.

> We had come so far from where we started, and weren't nearly approaching where we had to be, but we were on the road to becoming better.
>
> —Maya Angelou, *A Song Flung Up to Heaven*

3

Just Don't Tell Me I Can't!

Sandra Lowery by Sandra Harris

Parents don't send us the worst kids they have, they send us the best kids they have.

—Sandra Lowery

"**W**ell, it's probably 9:30 P.M. somewhere on the planet. Let's go home." In a few minutes, a rather small woman with short black hair streaked with gray walked out of the classroom surrounded by four or five men, all laughing and talking animatedly. Tonight, Dr. Sandra Lowery had been teaching a class of aspiring East Texas superintendents about school finance. Tomorrow night, she would be leading the Grapeland Independent School District Board of Education meeting as president of the school board.

The appointment of Sandra Lowery as chair of the Secondary Education and Educational Leadership Department at Stephen F. Austin State University and her election as the first female president of the school board in Grapeland, Texas, would have come as quite a surprise to Sandra's high school counselor nearly 40 years ago. In 1960, Sandra had moved to Texas with her parents and brother, but when she tried to enroll as a high school senior, the counselor had recommended that she drop out of school and find a job.

THE EARLY YEARS

Sandra started school in Louisiana when she was 5 years old. While she no longer remembers her teacher's name, she vividly remembers the two-story brick school building. Each morning her mother and younger brother would walk her to school, and then, in the afternoon, they would meet her in front of the building to walk home. Often, when Sandra got home from school, she would play "teacher" and try to coerce her brother to be her student. Like most younger brothers, he was not particularly interested in playing school, so most of her play teaching consisted of reading aloud to an imaginary class and developing a grade book, complete with a list of students and grades. Even as a 5-year-old, Sandra thought she might like to be a teacher someday.

Sandra's father worked as a pipeline welder and the family moved frequently, every few months at least. Consequently, she attended many schools every year. For example, from the 9th through the 11th grades, she attended schools in Mississippi, Texas, Louisiana, New Mexico, Kansas, and Oregon—nine schools altogether in just 3 years. It was not until the 12th grade that her desire to become a teacher was fueled, all because she was told that she should quit school.

When Sandra tried to enroll at an East Texas high school as a senior, she only had two half credits in foreign language. She had started her junior year in Louisiana, where the foreign language offered was French; then when the family had moved to New Mexico, Spanish was the language offered. The counselor at the new high school insisted that she would have to enroll as a junior and go an extra year because of her lack of foreign language credits. Sandra was crushed. The counselor knew that she was living with her grandmother in a poor neighborhood. But even though Sandra insisted that she had to finish high school this year, the counselor said that under no circumstances could she enroll as a senior. Then, she peered at Sandra over her white plastic reading glasses and added, "I seriously doubt that you would be able to make the grade at this school anyway since we have a rigorous academic program. I suggest that you drop out of school and get a job."

When Sandra went home and told her grandmother what had happened, her grandmother had said, "You can't let someone tell you that you can't do what you know you can." Her grandmother then proceeded to call every small school in the county to see if they would take transfers, and they all did. So Sandra rode with her cousin 15 miles every day to a new high school. She even got a job at a grocery store on Saturdays stocking groceries so that she could pay for her ride to school. Finally, for the first time in her life, as a senior, Sandra attended the same school for the whole year.

Years later, Sandra held the very position as the counselor who had advised her to quit high school. She had managed in spite of the counselor's advice not only to graduate from high school but also to graduate from university. She promised herself on the day that she moved into that same position that she would never advise a student to drop out of school. And she never did.

BECOMING AN EDUCATOR

One day, when Sandra was a senior in high school, an elementary teacher was ill for several days, and the school superintendent said that he needed her to help with the classroom. She recalls, "I jumped at it. Can you imagine how honored I felt? I loved it!" After Sandra graduated from high school, she considered the careers that were available to her: secretary, nurse, and teacher. Nursing was "not my thing. Teaching required a university degree, and I had married after high school, and soon had my first son." So she completed a secretarial course at a business college and went to work as a bookkeeper, but "making change in a hurry in front of customers was not a skill that I had, and besides I really wanted to teach." One evening, when her first son was 14 months old, the local school superintendent came to their home and offered her a job as teacher aide/ library aide/secretary for the local school district. He pointed out that this would be a much better job for her and her family. He also suggested that she "take every opportunity to complete your degree and teach."

Sandra enjoyed working at the school as an aide. Soon, the district had a new school superintendent, who suggested to her that "as a wife and mother with two sons, you'll make a good teacher." Sandra agreed and completed her degree in elementary education to become a teacher. After all, she had always wanted to teach.

In 1973, Sandra was pregnant with her third son, but she decided it was time to go back to school to earn her master's degree in hopes of becoming a school principal. However, she was discouraged from earning her master's in educational administration. After all, her superintendent reminded her, "Most women don't become administrators." Consequently, she became certified in supervision instead. But her desire to become a principal, and perhaps, one day, a superintendent, would not go away. In 1976, Sandra was admitted to Baylor University to earn her EdD in educational administration. She graduated as Dr. Sandra Lowery in 1978, and by that time she recalls "my burning desire was to become a superintendent, partly because I kept hearing that I couldn't."

DEVELOPING A LEADERSHIP STYLE

In addition to being a teacher and central office administrator, Sandra served as elementary principal, high school principal, and superintendent. Although her most recent education positions have been at the university and as school board president, she recalls those administrative positions with a special fondness as she became more comfortable with her own leadership style.

Learning to Be Collaborative

When Sandra talks about her first years as an elementary principal, she points out that she was not very collaborative:

> As an elementary [principal], I guess I thought I had to have all the answers and tell the teachers what to do and see that they did it. I came off that plan pretty quickly as, fortunately, I soon realized immediately that most of those ladies were excellent teachers who knew their stuff and they did not need, and certainly did not want, me trying to dictate to them. We began to be a team.

Sandra loved being an elementary principal and quickly learned about student discipline, working with parents, and how to move an entire school from one location to another. In fact, the day after she was hired, the school burned. She remembers thinking, "Oh, no, we can't have school without our building . . . we can't do this." But they did. That school year until the next Christmas holiday, the elementary faculty held school in portable buildings. Then the elementary faculty packed again and moved into the old three-story junior high building that had originally been a high school. Even today she remembers the sense of family and community that was built as a result of the fire. Coaches, teachers, maintenance staff, high school students, the superintendent, her husband, and her youngest son, Brad, all helped with the moves. She laughs as she recalls how each day at noon, the superintendent brought hamburgers, french fries, and soft drinks for all the workers. The last day they worked on the move, her son Brad, who was about 11 years old at the time, told the superintendent, "Mr. Murray, we are sure gonna miss those hamburgers!"

Learning to Be More Open

Even in the late 1970s, few women became high school principals, and Sandra had been told that this was something she "could not expect to do." But, nevertheless, she was appointed high school principal. This was a special challenge because Sandra had never taught in a high school. Again, she quickly realized that the teachers knew about curriculum; she decided that it was her role to discipline students, work with parents, and oversee extracurricular activities. There was no assistant principal, but the athletic director had pointed out just before she was hired that "this high school principal job is a two-handed job," meaning that it would be a demanding position. The superintendent of the school district helped her with this steep learning curve. He insisted that she could do this job better than anyone else. He also never judged her mistakes and was willing to assist her when she needed his help. He knew that she wanted to be a superintendent and that being a high school principal was a much better route than being an elementary principal at the time, especially for women.

As a high school principal, Sandra became more comfortable with being a collaborative leader. She also became more comfortable in dealing openly and directly with others. She remembers that she never had to go through nonrenewal with a teacher, but she counseled several out of education. Even though she "never reached a point where it didn't just tear me up inside, I never made that move unless I sincerely believed it was absolutely necessary for the students. Once I reached that point, I could look a teacher in the eye and tell them to find another job."

Sandra also worked at developing strong relationships with parents. Often, she told anxious parents of high school students who were giving teachers and parents a hard time, "You know, I watched lots of kids finally grow up and become reasonable adults who raised good families and are solid citizens today." Not only was this true, but as parents were comforted, they also developed a renewed respect for school leaders. She also encouraged teachers not to be judgmental of parenting skills and would tell teachers, "Parents don't send us the worst kids they have, they send us the best kids they have."

THE CHALLENGE OF THE SUPERINTENDENCY

Sandra wanted to be a superintendent, and she applied for many positions, but the coveted job kept eluding her. Still, she was confident that if she could just get the opportunity, she would be a good superintendent. She laughs and quotes an East Texas saying that "a blind hog finds an acorn once in a while; so I knew that if I just kept applying, eventually I would be hired as a superintendent." And she was.

Sandra held three superintendencies during the 1980s and early 1990s; in each case she was the first female hired to fill this district leadership position, and they all provided challenging learning experiences. She modeled many of her leadership skills after the superintendents with whom she had worked. For example, she remembers how the superintendent who had hired her as an elementary and high school principal listened, encouraged, and assisted. He might not have called his leadership style *collaborative*, but it was. But the job itself was so demanding that she describes the workday as "pretty much can 'til can't."

Being Called "the Skirt"

In her first superintendency she found herself in a challenging position. The male coaches in the district had all strongly supported the hiring of a man within the district, and they were not shy about letting her know that. She was immediately named "the Skirt." She smiles now as she remembers some of the difficulties of that first year and then says, "But don't tell me I can't!" So, she focused on improving the school academically and building relationships. She even had the audacity to call in the athletic director and inform him that the school would not pay for anything unless he had a purchase order. After the 10th time of arguing with him and paying his bills without a purchase order,

> I stood my ground . . . no, I stood the school's ground, . . . and the next time he submitted a bill without a purchase order . . . it was not paid by the school. Soon, I overcame being afraid of making a decision, and we began building, remodeling, and improving student performance in many ways. I was actually leading the district with the help of a supportive community.

Standing Up for Herself

The second superintendency was in a much larger school district. Sandra was recommended for the position because her reputation for being able to work with people and bring the community together was growing. She was hired and given a 3-year contract. When the board conducted the annual superintendent evaluation, she was given an excellent evaluation. But when she requested an extended contract, they said, "You have done a wonderful job, the teachers respect you, you have straightened up things in the transportation department, you are a good manager of the budget, . . . but we have decided that we just do not believe in 3-year contracts, so we want to let your original 3-year contract run out and we'll talk about a new contract then." She would not make the hard decisions and tread water daily in the political atmosphere of the superintendency without the security of a contract. A friend later told her that several board members thought that she would not have the backbone to stand up to the board. They were stunned when she told them that night that she would be looking for another job.

Gaining Confidence

Sandra's third superintendency was in a small, troubled district very close to her family's home. It had recently undergone leadership problems so serious that the state department of education had appointed a master to oversee the district. But in her own words,

> I came into this position with a more defined perspective of leadership. I was the superintendent, and I had a stronger sense of my role and the board's role. We got along fine. We saved money for buildings, computers,

buses, and other things that the district really needed—paid cash for everything. We refined the concurrent credit program in the high school and part-
nered with a nearby community college—which they are still doing. My annual evaluations were excellent. The district was good to me, and I hope that
I was good for the district.

When Sandra resigned to take a position at a university, they did not want
to let her go. With Sandra as superintendent, this school district community had learned to trust again.

SACRIFICES AND CHALLENGES TO
BEING AN EDUCATIONAL LEADER

Being a full-time working wife and mother has often presented challenges
to Sandra. For example, there was little understanding in her small community in the early 1970s of her drive to become an educational leader.
She remembers a summer day when she was getting gas for her car for the
drive to Baylor University, nearly 150 miles away, to work on her doctoral
degree. Her two older sons, Mike and David, were staying at home and
her husband, Neil, was in charge of taking care of them. She rolled her
window down to tell the service station owner to fill up the car with gas.
As he did so, he commented, "This is some crazy idea, you going off to
get a doctorate."

There were family sacrifices. When Sandra started to attend graduate
school at Baylor University, there was no school board policy to allow her
to keep her teaching position at the elementary school. At the same time,
her husband resigned his principal position to become self-employed. So,
with three children and a newly self-employed husband, Sandra resigned
her teaching position to begin work on a doctoral degree. Some weeks,
she would go to Waco in time for a Tuesday night class, stay over for a
Wednesday night class, and then drive home, getting home about midnight. Neil and the boys ate a lot of canned chili and frozen french fries.
They managed, with everyone helping.

The first summer that Sandra was at Baylor, she rented a small apart-
ment near the campus and enrolled 3-year-old Brad in a nearby day care.
He cried when she took him in the morning, and he was crying when she

picked him up. This went on for 3 days, until finally, she told a friend that she was not going to be able to stay in summer school. Thankfully, that friend had a 13-year-old daughter who needed a summer job.

As a superintendent of small school districts, Sandra attended nearly every extracurricular activity. She was in the office before 8:00 A.M. and usually attended school activities Tuesday, Thursday, and Friday evenings and tournaments and other school activities on Saturdays. The community just expected to see the principals and superintendents at everything. But in addition to this being her job, she attended these events because she was interested in the communities and the students who attended the schools she led. Usually Neil and often her sons attended with her. But from the very beginning of her superintendency, Sandra knew that no job was worth sacrificing her family. In retrospect, she suggests that perhaps everyone working together may have actually contributed to her whole family's sense of responsibility for one another.

When Sandra accepted her first university teaching position, it was located over 150 miles away from her home. Once again, Neil and the boys were supportive. They ate out a lot, some weeks every evening. They also usually had household help. But as she reflects back on those busy days, Sandra admits that "most of the time we met ourselves coming and going." After 41 years of marriage, she considers her husband her greatest support and has wonderful relationships with her three sons and their families. She is especially proud of her grandchildren, Clint, Matthew, J. T., Garrett, and Sarah.

ON TO THE NEXT EDUCATIONAL LEADERSHIP CHALLENGES

In 1997, Sandra ran for the school board because she wanted to give something back to the educational system that had been so good to her over the years. She was elected. Having been a superintendent, she has an especially perceptive understanding of school board duties. She, more than most, understands that a board member's role is to lead through developing policy. She was especially honored when she was elected to serve as president of the board for 2 years.

During her role as president of the school board, Sandra was selected to become the department chair of the Secondary Education and Educational

Leadership Department for the university. Because of the tremendous time that this job required, she did not run for a second term on the school board. Instead, she threw her energies into leading a university department that prepares school administrators.

Over 30 years ago, a school counselor recommended that Sandra drop out of high school. Without an attitude that was able to embrace challenge, it is possible that Sandra Lowery might have become just one more high school dropout. Instead, she became a highly respected educator who has improved schools throughout Texas and has been recognized for her leadership as a teacher, principal, superintendent, school board member and president, and university leader. Without a hint of pride, but with much humility and self-humor, she laughs and says, "Don't tell me I can't, just encourage me that I can."

One can never consent to creep, when one feels an impulse to soar.

—Helen Keller

4

The Right Stuff: Living a Legacy of Leadership

Molly Helminger by Betty Alford

School is about white water rafting, not drifting on Golden Pond.

—Molly Helminger

In the movie *The Right Stuff* there is a scene where the commander in chief draws a diagram describing the point where the astronauts will run out of oxygen and the point of reentry to the atmosphere. The diagram shows a marked gap between the two points. He then turns to the engineers and says, "Failure is not an option." The determination characterized by this commander, who inspired a team to solve the problem for the astronauts' successful reentry to the atmosphere, is clearly evident in Molly Helminger's determination to truly "leave no child behind" in the schools she leads. Dr. Helminger, a petite 46-year-old powerhouse, leads a district as superintendent, always modeling the philosophy of "kids first." She is relentless in the quest to improve academic achievement through a team effort and disciplined data-driven actions. Requiring weekly progress reports, benchmark tests, and personnel evacuations tied to students' academic performance, Dr. Helminger tells her coworkers:

> Participation is not our option. We are here to compete. Like white water rafting, we will experience changes, but I'll serve as your guide in the lead boat while other campus administrators serve as the additional team leaders in the rafts that follow. We will probably ride these rapids for 2 years until we achieve our goals, but we will succeed.

Passion, determination, and commitment characterize Molly Helminger's words and actions. With high ethical principles, she moves each school that she leads from an accountability rating in the Texas State Accountability System of Acceptable to Exemplary, feats she has already accomplished in three districts in her 10 years as a superintendent and once in her previous role as a campus principal. Rising to the rank of superintendent by the age of 36 is an unusual accomplishment for a woman in Texas, where women are still in the minority in the role of school superintendent. However, though Molly ascended to the leading role in a district at a young age, she entered this realm of school leadership with a strong knowledge base and a grounded personal philosophy influenced by cumulative experiences in multitask roles that provided a rich K–12 perspective, as well as educational preparation through the completion of two master's degrees and a doctoral degree.

WHAT CONTRIBUTES TO MOLLY'S EFFECTIVENESS AS A SCHOOL LEADER?

Factors that contribute to Molly Helminger's effectiveness as a school leader include her preparation in her early years, faith, communication skills, use of power, disciplined life, and knowledge of the school improvement process.

Early Years

Molly Helminger was the sixth of seven children and lived in a single-parent household from the age of 6. Her father, a teacher, coach, and ex-Marine, died from cancer when Molly was only 6, leaving her mother, a teacher, to raise seven children, aged 5, 6, 7, 8, 9, 10, and 11. Molly's mother established the nonnegotiable rule that every child would compete in at least one sport and learn one musical instrument. In fact, Molly's mother emphasized that the question was not "whether" she would participate but "which will you pursue to excellence?" Money that was spent on lessons and trips to practice was not to be wasted by inattention. Practice was expected, as was diligence to the task at hand. Molly's mother told her, "Your jobs are to study and to practice piano, viola, and athletics!"

Molly began taking viola lessons at 6 and piano at age 5, the same year she began to train for athletic competition in track. While accompanying her older sister to track practice, the coach noticed Molly's athletic talent and convinced her mother to allow her to begin training. This training kindled a love of running that has continued to the present. Despite an extremely busy schedule, Molly continues to work out for an hour each morning, to work out with a trainer twice a week, and to run competitively. In a 4A high school, she excelled in basketball, volleyball, and softball in addition to track.

Molly's musical and athletic talents were accompanied by strong academic skills, and this combination led to Molly's career choice to become a music teacher and athletic coach, an unusual combination that provided a tremendous opportunity to work with a wide range of students and parents. Molly taught for 5 years, during which time she also earned a master's degree in guidance and counseling. Told that she would need to wait probably 5 years before an opening for a counselor would be present in the district, she decided to move to another district. However, she broadened her range of experiences. With six siblings living in Texas, California, Washington, and Florida, she decided to select a state near one of her sisters. That state was Texas.

The decision to come to Texas was a strategic one because Molly knew she wanted to obtain her doctorate in educational leadership. She accepted a school counseling position in a 2A district near Texas Tech University and worked as a counselor and at other positions for 5 years while also completing her doctoral studies. As a counselor, she had no disciplinary responsibilities and was able to build a strong developmental guidance program for K–12 with a focus on best practices. While completing her doctoral work, Molly worked with the Texas Association of School Boards and surveyed over 3,000 trustees and educators. This helped in furthering her understanding of policy issues from a statewide perspective.

The superintendent where Molly was working as a counselor recognized her talents and asked her to serve as elementary school principal without an interview or even an application. He simply stated, "You're going to be a leader." Surprised but pleased by the offer, she accepted the position and immediately began working to improve students' academic performance, in turn developing skills in the school improvement process that would become her trademark. In 3 years, she moved the campus from Low Performing to Recognized and eventually to Exemplary.

Faith

Faith is a foundation of Molly's personal philosophy. She gains strength from her faith and believes God has given her strong character, energy, intensity, and talent, though it is up to her to develop her strengths. A catalyst for her work is a belief in destiny, in short, a higher calling she defines as "to leave behind a legacy of leaders." This destiny influences Molly's strong belief in the importance of teamwork and the development of talent in the district. Just as an administrator noticed her talent and moved her to a primary campus leadership role of principal, she looks for talent in others and assigns these outstanding individuals to key leadership roles.

A big part of Molly's day is spent coaching and mentoring principals and other school leaders. In the role of a mentor and coach to others as a strong school leader, criticism can also arise. When difficulties arise, her faith sustains her to remain focused on "kids first" as an educational philosophy on which to base all decisions. In Molly's office is a statement she strongly believes, "Each of us is a secret that God makes public." She explains, "Unless grounded in faith, a leader's ethical focus can become distorted." Molly readily reveals that faith is a large part of her life and of her early years. In her family, one sister became a nun while her brother became a priest. Molly laughs and adds, "I might as well be" a nun, in reference to her choice to remain single.

Responsibility is much more than a word to Molly. It is a catalyst for action. "Pace harder," she proclaims, adding that she believes strongly in developing one's self mentally, physically, and spiritually in response to God's abiding love. An attribute she seeks in other school leaders is courage, particularly courage to do what is unpopular if the decision is in the best interest of students. Faith keeps her grounded and provides her course of action. Failure is not an option in Molly's view. When disappointments arise, her faith provides her with the strength to begin again.

Communication Skills

Another contributing factor to Molly's effectiveness as a school leader is her strong communication skills. With training as a school counselor, Molly is adept at listening closely to discern what is really being said, and she understands that some communication should be public while some discussions need to remain private. Communication that must be public is the constant communication of the key goals for school improvement. "It is important for faculty, community members, board trustees, parents, and other administrators to internalize the vision of true success for every child," Molly emphasizes. "For this to occur, the leader must repeatedly champion the cause."

One way that Molly brings this vision of success for every child to life is through the use of analogies. She describes the school improvement process as one of riding the rapids. She explains, "Guides are important, but riding the rapids is difficult, as is achieving change. The waters will eventually calm after the rapids have been crossed; however, while going through the rapids [change process], it is natural to experience stress." Molly is convinced that the trip through the rapids is easier as a team with guides and coaches rather than entering uncharted water alone. She reminds faculty that "we are white water rafting, not drifting on Golden Pond."

Analogies such as that of the white water river rafting are a powerful communication tool. Other communication tools that Molly uses include cultivating the media to assist in sharing the good news about the district and also accepting public speaking engagements, such as a presentation to the Regional Council of School Boards. Molly is highly visible in the district, visiting campuses weekly and attending two or three school extracurricular events each night of scheduled events. Her communication is primarily face to face. In fact she relates, "My secretary checks my e-mail messages. Don't e-mail if you want an answer from me."

While meeting with the public, Molly repeatedly shares her unwavering belief that academic improvement must be first in a school district and that the quality of a child's experience can make a tremendous difference in a child's life. "Quality appreciates quality," she often says. She further adds, "When we work to achieve a high-quality education for every child, our work is appreciated and a source of pride; and quality individuals want to apply to work in the district, and quality individuals want to remain."

Use of Power

Molly believes, "There is power in empowering others." She further explains, "In school leadership, there are tidal waves. We are bombarded by data. My role is to teach others how to ride the waves."

In Molly's view, school leadership is a rigorous task. "The leader must refuse to allow fellow educators not to pace hard. If we are losing students, we must jump in and save them." Molly's leadership style is collaborative yet direct. She believes that leaders must "look people in the eye, do the homework in studying the needs of the school, and work to achieve outstanding results." She adds, "I shoot straight and don't mince words." As she explains, "I don't want to show administrators and teachers the door if they aren't working hard to improve the schools, but I will if I need to. Also, I will provide them the opportunity to open up their own futures."

Molly's forthrightness is grounded in her knowledge of self. Molly stresses, "I am who I am. I believe a person must know who he or she is, what they value and believe as well as their nonnegotiables, the things they will not compromise." She quickly adds, "Every student's success is our number one priority at our school district. The strength of leadership is a person's ability to coach and mentor others." To Molly, the bottom line is not about power, "the bottom line is that a leader has to have the courage from within and has to be a team player." Molly stresses that an important element of collaborative power is the establishment of trust.

In working with the school board, she views her job as "to lead the team of eight in quality decision making for the well-being of the entire school district." Molly continues her description of school leadership with an analogy of the United Nations, stating that though the United Nations represents separate countries, the countries act as a unit when important measures are passed. She stresses that every 3 to 5 years, the school board must review and revise policy to support the school improvement process.

In the process of personnel decision making, Molly recommends that the superintendent inform the school board, as well as employees, that renewal of contracts will be aligned with student performance. One of her primary responsibilities is ensuring that the board of trustees understand that part of the school improvement process requires putting the right people in the right positions for maximum results. For Molly, replacing ineffective personnel is a nonnegotiable. "If students are repeatedly failing in a school, then there is a problem with personnel," she argues, "and tough decisions must be made." Molly believes it is important that the board of trustees endorse this view if this philosophy is to guide the superintendent's actions in a district.

She further recommends that the superintendent and the school board "always work to become a team of eight—not puppets of one another but united in the quest of higher achievement for all students, consistently asking, 'Where do we want to see the school district in 5 years?'" In summary, she stresses, "Always communicate, communicate, and communicate in a chain of service, not a chain of command."

Disciplined Life

A fifth contributing factor to Molly's success is her disciplined life. Believing that talent was not meant to be wasted, she is up at 5:00 A.M. each morning for exercise and is at work by 7:00 A.M. Though not a vegetarian, she primarily eats vegetables and fruits, eliminating sugars and minimizing the intake of meat. Training as a runner is a disciplined activity, and she brings this discipline to her daily life where her philosophy and actions are inherently entwined. With a belief that one must be all that he or she can be, her actions translate to a disciplined diet and exercise plan. This discipline carries over to the school improvement process with an emphasis on data analysis. A strong statistician who loves studying school data and finance, she encourages other school leaders to know the school through analysis of the data, asking, "How are we doing in each area and subarea and among each subpopulation?" She adds, "Being good overall is not good enough." Molly believes that schools must strive to achieve the rating of Exemplary and use the statewide testing data as a minimum benchmark standard of performance. Disciplined, ongoing analysis of school data is an important part of Molly's work.

Molly admits that she may be seen as a workaholic. But she quickly adds, "I don't expect everyone to be like me. But I do expect 100% effort during the workday and recognize that a school administrator's job is probably going to be from 7:00 A.M. to 7:00 P.M. at a minimum."

Knowledge of the School Improvement Process

A final contributing factor to Molly's effectiveness as a school leader is her strong knowledge of key elements in the school improvement process. As previously mentioned, Molly understands the importance of clear communication of the vision and of the importance of ongoing data analysis in the process of school improvement. She recognizes fully that changes should be made in response to clear needs and that an important part of a faculty's willingness to embrace change is whether or not they have clearly articulated the need that is prompting the change. She knows that success in the school improvement process is apparent when increasing numbers of faculty, administrators, and staff are articulating the vision, making improvements based on analysis of the data and clearly identified needs, and exhibiting a clear sense of urgency to the tasks at hand. In addition, Molly recognizes the importance of being an authentic leader and modeling the behavior expected of others.

Molly's experiences as a coach and musician have influenced her belief that excellence is achieved through focused work. The school improvement process is difficult, as is running a marathon or playing the viola (both endeavors she pursues), but there is also exhilaration in the achievement of goals. As a school leader, Molly has experienced the accomplishment of moving campuses from Low Performing or Acceptable to Exemplary. She knows the school improvement process takes time (at least 2 years) and hard work, but by having accomplished this as superintendent of three school districts, she knows the goals can be achieved "in both incremental steps and quantum leaps," and she "thrives on the challenge."

The goals for her district are to be nationally recognized in leadership, academics, curriculum, and technology. Toward achieving these results, ongoing data analysis is an important first step in the improvement of academic skills. Second, facilitating curriculum alignment to ensure that all students are prepared for the Texas Assessment of Knowledge and Skills (TAKS) is a necessity, with benchmark testing every 6 weeks. Technology serves as a tool for the preparation of weekly academic progress reports for each core subject area for students, and these reports are signed by parents of elementary school children and by students in secondary schools. Teachers are required to take a minimum number of grades each 9 weeks, and technology also assists as a tool in computer grade reporting so that grades can be provided to parents with a push of the button. The strong push for academic excellence is supported by rescheduling students who are not passing core subjects from the elective classes to accelerated classes for intense work in those core areas. In addition, mandatory summer school is required for students in grades 3 to 8 who do not have at least a 70 average in core subjects by the end of the year or who fail any sections of the TAKS. These strategies represent a few of the factors that Molly has implemented in the school improvement process.

WHAT IGNITES MOLLY'S PASSION?

Concern for students' growth academically, spiritually, and physiologically ignites Molly's passion. Recognizing fully the importance of separation of church and state, she restricts religious teaching to the children's Sunday school class that she leads. But she is quick to point out that there is more to the spiritual side of life than the study of doctrine. "When children are given hugs in elementary school and encouraged to reach to new heights, this, too, is a part of a child's spiritual development," Molly explains.

With Molly there are many nonnegotiables, "about 80%," she says. However, these nonnegotiables are not related to strict rules but instead to aspects of caring that simply must be demonstrated by effective educators. The school improvement process requires courage and passion to improve schools so that each child can truly succeed. Molly has internalized this descriptor of the school improvement process and demonstrates it daily in her work. She reflectively sets in motion plans for school improvement, consistently setting goals and reaching them.

WHAT HAVE BEEN MOLLY'S OBSTACLES?

Molly identifies three primary obstacles she has had to overcome in her quest to be a leader: schools not ready for female leaders, districts not prepared for female leaders, and loneliness.

Schools Not Ready for Female Leaders

As Molly explains, "Just as rapids serve as obstacles on a river raft ride, obstacles can and do appear for educational leaders involved in the school improvement process." Early in her career, Molly was informed that the school was not ready for a woman leader. She accepted this obstacle as reality but, simply, sought a new path just as though going around a boulder in the river when rafting. Molly sought employment in a different district during that year while strengthening her administrative skills through the position of assistant superintendent. She recommends to other women, "When it is time to move on, move on. Don't waste time."

Districts Not Prepared for Female Leaders

Molly acknowledges that women superintendents are still in the minority in schools. "To rise to this position," Molly explains, "a woman must be clearly outstanding." Molly prepared for the role of superintendent through assuming many K–12 diverse responsibilities, such as appraising K–12 teachers and teaching and coaching K–12. Small schools afforded her the opportunity to quickly acquire skills at all levels, though her own background in a large high school also provided the perspective of a large school setting. "Women must be well prepared to compete, and a doctorate degree is becoming more widely accepted as an entry requirement for many school superintendents' positions, regardless of gender," she asserts.

Loneliness

Another obstacle for women can be the loneliness of being one of few women in top positions. The support network can often be small. However, part of the way Molly has overcome this obstacle is through her faith and her high involvement in district activities.

When Molly considered her own obstacles, she recommended five strategies for women leaders. Molly emphasizes that women should be "encouraged to not accept limits, set goals, develop a plan, climb to great heights, but always remember who you are" in their quest to be effective leaders.

CONCLUSION

Focus and discipline grounded in faith and manifested in high energy and positive actions are Molly's trademarks. With this combination, she has continued to rise in the educational field, having already served as a school superintendent for 10 years by the age of 46. The board of trustees have described her as a "powerful presence, intense, passionate, and a fireball."

As I walked away from our interview, the message that resonated within my soul was that the path is not for the fainthearted, but we can all rise to achieve our dreams, whatever those dreams may be. I was reminded that we create our legacy as we live. It is not something simply that is left when we are gone. Pausing again to consider the movie *The Right Stuff*, which illuminated aspects of astronauts' training, knowledge, character, and skills that prepared them for the task at hand, I thought of Molly as another equal to the descriptor "the right stuff." She stands as a school leader who represents our highest ideals and is, indeed, living a legacy of leadership.

> The great thing in this world is not so much where we stand as in what direction we are moving.
>
> —Oliver Wendell Holmes

***

> What you are is God's gift to you; what you make of yourself is your gift to God.
>
> —George Washington Carver

5

The Trailblazer

Donnya Stephens by Julia Ballenger

Stumbling blocks can impede our progress or they can give us the motivation to march on. Choose to march on.

—Donnya Stephens

It was a beautiful fall morning in East Texas. As I turned left onto College Street I could see the university nestled among the tall and stately pine trees. I parked in my usual parking place and walked quickly up the sidewalk to the McKibben Education Building. I stepped out of the elevator on the fourth floor, feeling somewhat nervous about my upcoming interview with Dr. Donnya Stephens.

Dr. Stephens had taught at the university for 27 years, earning numerous honors for her scholarship and services to the university and community. I walked past the Wall of Fame displayed near the office of the dean of the College of Education. Donnya was the only African American professor at the university whose awards were displayed with other outstanding professors. She was truly a trailblazer in higher education as well as in the K–12 public school system. Her awards included Regents Professor, Distinguished Alumni Professor, Phi Delta Kappa Educator of the Year, Woman of the Year for the American Association of University Women, Top Ladies of Distinction award, and induction into the Texas Women's Hall of Fame for Education. The thought of interviewing Donnya was both a humbling and a proud experience for me.

Donnya's beautiful, inviting smile immediately put me at ease. She directed me toward a comfortable chair. I looked around her office and saw many other plaques demonstrating outstanding achievement and community service, such as Nacogdoches Women's Hall of Fame, United Way, Community Action, Head Start, and Nacogdoches Adult Literacy. I could not help but notice that she was the only person of color in all of the pictures displayed in her office. She brought me back to the present by stating, "I'm so grateful that you chose to allow my 'voice' to be heard among the many outstanding women leaders." Donnya was eager to share her story about women's issues ranging from family support, racial and gender barriers, and mentors to successful strategies she used as she climbed the ladder to success. She was eager to have her often courageous personal and professional experiences recorded to encourage other women to succeed regardless of obstacles encountered. Donnya's story begins with her early childhood experiences, which laid the foundation for the successful, courageous woman she would become.

EARLY CHILDHOOD EXPERIENCES

Young African American girls, including this interviewer, spent many days playing the role of the teacher with our cousins and friends. We taught Sunday school classes in our local churches and tutored many of the slower learning students in school. Most of our role models were teachers; therefore, we dreamed of becoming a teacher. But to my amazement, this master teacher, Donnya Stephens, did not select the field of teaching as a career choice. Instead, Donnya speaks frankly about her desire to become a secretary. "To be honest with you, I had no desire to become a teacher in my early years. I used to watch the *I Love Lucy* show on television. I really wanted to be a secretary."

Donnya's mother was an English teacher and later became a curriculum director in a public school district. She encouraged her daughter to become a teacher, but Donnya admits that "for some reason, I wanted to do something different."

Donnya recalls the significance of her mother in her life as a recurring theme:

My mother told me that I needed to get a teaching certificate. She said, "Girl, there are only two places in this area [segregated East Texas] where you will be able to get a job as a secretary, and that is at one of the two African American mortuaries and insurance agencies."

During the segregation era, job opportunities were limited, and in the early 1950s and 1960s, African American girls were counseled to become teachers or secretaries. Public schools and African American businesses, such as insurance agencies, mortuaries, and the one or two local doctor's offices, offered few job opportunities for African American women.

Several experiences during Donnya's early childhood shaped her future work ethic and value for an education. She recalls how

as a teacher's child, I had to work much harder than the other children. I had to be better than they were in order to achieve anything. I had to make sure that people felt I earned whatever I achieved. I did not feel good about those early experiences as a teacher's child. I was also told that as an African American I had to be twice as good as the white children to compete on a level playing field with them.

Donnya's maternal grandmother also helped shape her future work ethic and her value for education.

When I started elementary school my mother taught out of town. The children lived with my grandmother 5 days a week and with my parents on the weekend. My grandmother only had a fifth-grade education; however, it was important to her that we got an education. Every afternoon when we would come in from school, we would go and work in the fields if it was crop time. We would get our baths in a number 3 tub. After our baths, my grandmother would tell us to study our lesson. Sometimes we would say to her that we had gotten our lesson at school. She would tell us to sit down and hold the book for an hour. When you have to hold a book for an hour by a kerosene lamp, for some reason, you find yourself preferring to read the book rather than just holding it.

Donnya reflects a moment and smiles as she shares her grandmother's unforgettable influence on her life.

My grandmother often told me, "I didn't get an education, but you are going to get one." She was determined that I would get an education. If the roads were too muddy for the school bus to run, my grandmother put rubber boots on our feet and carried our shoes so that we didn't miss a day of school for any reason.

Donnya learned two important lessons from her early childhood experiences: You don't have to live in a household of educators to learn the value of an education, and hard work won't kill you. In fact, working hard was one of the essential elements of her success. The family practices in Donnya's home were more important than the family structure in providing her with a strong work ethic and excellent academic foundation. As she continued to give her story voice, it was clear that these core values and work ethic helped make her the successful educator she is today.

UNIQUE ENTRY INTO TEACHING

After graduating from a small rural segregated public school, Donnya chose to attend one of the largest African American colleges in Texas. During the early 1950s, colleges were still segregated. Donnya's goal was to major in business education and find a husband. She was fortunate to obtain a job working in the business office to help pay for her college education. During Donnya's senior year in college, she was asked to teach a freshman English class. She accepted the offer with the chance of earning more money. As a result of her success with this freshman English class, her appetite for teaching grew. Donnya graduated with a degree . . . but she did not find a husband.

Donnya's entry into teaching was unique. It was her mother who influenced her to enter the teaching profession.

> I graduated from college in May. I spent the summer working in a hospital cafeteria. My job was picking up trays after the patients finished their meals. I also helped the cafeteria staff with washing dishes. The fall was fast approaching. I had not applied for a professional job. My mother told me that if I didn't get a professional job by the fall, I would have to return to college. I didn't want to return to college. A friend of mine told me about a teaching job in East Texas.

So Donnya rode a bus to the little town in East Texas for her first teaching interview, where she was offered the job as an English teacher in a segregated high school.

After 12 years of successful teaching experience in the public schools, Donnya was offered a teaching position at a local junior college. She was the only woman of color in the department. While teaching at the junior college, she encountered several barriers. Her supervisor did not recruit her. Her work was monitored often. Therefore Donnya felt that she was not fully embraced as a member of the department. But she did not let the lack of connection to the supervisor keep her from working hard and becoming an effective teacher. She improved her teaching skills by studying hard, and she earned a master's degree. After teaching for 2 years at the junior college, she was invited to teach at the local university. Donnya's early work ethic had paved the way for her success. She worked hard, and her outstanding performance caused others to seek her out for employment. With gracious humility, but just a touch of pride, Donnya admits, "I've never applied for a job that I have not gotten. My performance speaks for itself."

Donnya Stephens did not enter the teaching profession because she wanted to be a teacher or because she selected the job of teaching; she was called. She accepted this call to become a teacher and never looked back. Donnya's success as a master teacher can be attributed to her strong work ethic, her commitment to academic success, her personality, and her success with managing students.

DONNYA'S SUCCESS WITH STUDENTS

Donnya worked at building a supportive and caring relationship with her students.

> I wanted to make a difference in the lives of my students. I never had any difficulty in connecting with my students. I was always available. I was approachable, and I was patient with them. I spent many hours conferencing with students in my office after class, listening to their problems and concerns. Therefore, I took a lot of work home every night. I felt that nothing else mattered at that time except to spend the time with the students. They just wanted someone to listen to them.

Even now, 27 years since Donnya first began teaching, students are always seen in her office or waiting in the hallway to visit with her. When

Donnya describes her relationship as a teacher with her students, she notes that

> I am a caring and nurturing person. I play fairly. I did not have discipline prob-
> lems in my classroom. I established the kind of mutual respect that is impor-
> tant in order to be successful in the classroom. Students, especially African
> American, respond positively to teachers who show that they care about them.

Donnya Stephens is passionately committed to the belief that effective teachers model caring, nurturing behaviors—and this is how she teaches. She began teaching this way in a public high school classroom, and it continues today in her university classroom. Her appealing persona attracts students to her. They know that she is genuine and committed to helping all her students.

Donnya describes an early teaching experience that blazed a trail for her success from a high school classroom to the university:

> During my senior year in college, I had a freshman class of athletes. I did
> not have classroom management problems. Students knew that I had their
> best interest at heart. I tried to treat them with respect. During my first year
> of teaching in public school, I was quite young. I had to clearly delineate
> my standards for appropriate behavior in the classroom. The students lived
> up to my standards. I got to know the students' parents and involved them
> in their children's school activities. I visited their homes and got to know
> the students and parents on a personal level.

Donnya not only treats all students with respect but also sets high expectations for their academic success. Even as a young teacher, Donnya Stephens knew that setting high expectations for all students is an essential characteristic of an effective teacher. She also determined that to do this effectively she would be caring and strive to meet the needs of all students.

DONNYA'S LEADERSHIP STYLES

As Donnya describes her leadership style, she quickly states, "I lead from behind. I don't have to be the center of attention." Capturing the essence of her leadership style, she points out:

I do not have to be out front all the time. I get satisfaction in seeing that the work is completed and it is completed right. I don't have to get the credit for the work I do. I am concerned with quality and being inclusive; I value including others. Although I have not had an official administrative position, I did serve as program coordinator at the university for 6 years. I used the participatory and collaborative style of leadership. I recognize the expertise of others with whom I work. So I include them in the decision-making process regarding issues that affect them directly.

Donnya shares the following incidents that further describe her leadership skills and continue to illuminate the influence of her work ethic:

At the university we are constantly revising the structure and curriculum of our secondary education program. We [all instructors] worked together as a team to restructure the program. I shared the work with everyone. As a result we developed an outstanding program that we presented at several national conferences.

Another situation involves conducting the ExCET [mandated Texas teacher certification exam] reviews on Saturdays. I knew that the instructors had families and didn't want to spend their entire Saturday working. I allowed the instructors to provide the review for a few hours during the morning. I would come up on Saturday evenings and give the test so that they would not have to give up all of their Saturday. I did this to show them that I valued their time. They were the ones getting the financial compensation; I did not receive any financial compensation. This was part of the responsibility of being a coordinator.

Donnya also believes in the importance of working closely with new university professors. She often visits them to find out what materials or help they might need. She shares her materials, lesson units, and textbooks with them. She also invites them to "serve on department and university committees so that they will learn about higher education and get to network with other faculty throughout the university." Helping beginning faculty focus their careers toward gaining tenure is also important to Donnya.

Those who work with Donnya comment that she "understands people." She is aware of their needs and strengths. Donnya points out that she knows "the professors who need leadership responsibilities and those who are good team members." She praises and encourages new professors often.

BARRIERS ENCOUNTERED

Our conversation moved from leadership styles to barriers. Realizing that Donnya was a trailblazer and often the only African American female in the workplace, I asked her if she would share any racial or gender biases that she had experienced. Donnya had successfully obtained both master's and doctoral degrees. She was honored by being on the university's Wall of Fame. The wall of her office is covered with plaques and awards honoring her achievements. But her voice cracks when I ask about barriers, and I can see tears in her eyes. Both of us pause, each of us remembering the struggles we have faced during our path to leadership. After what seemed like an eternity, Donnya responded to the question:

> When I first came to the university as an instructor, most people thought I was working for a federal program that dealt with diversity; they didn't think I was a professor at the university. I was one of two African American professors at the university in the mid-70s [the other African American professor was male]. I was looked upon as an African American female professor to the faculty and to my students. Every day I walked into the classroom I had to prove to my students that I was worthy of having this position. The students told me that I was the first African American professor they had ever had at high school or college. Once the students learned that I knew my subject matter and was fair to all of them, I gained credibility.

Because Donnya was the only African American woman professor on campus, she was invited to serve on numerous committees. However, Donnya experienced yet other barriers while working on committees. She recalls that

> I served on numerous committees throughout the university. However, I was not heard or recognized for my academic abilities. I would make a statement in the meeting, but no one would acknowledge it. It was just like I was not present. A few minutes later a white professor would make a similar statement, and everyone would acknowledge and accept the statement.

Donnya felt that her acceptance was strictly on a social level, as a representative for women and African Americans. She shares how other professors complimented her on her appearance but not on her academic accomplishments. When I asked how she coped with this lack of acceptance, she reflected on her early childhood experiences:

> I grew up quite comfortable with who I was and what I had achieved. My mother always taught me that I was just as capable as anyone else. I knew that I had to work harder than others just to be on a level playing ground with them, but I was used to hard work.

Donnya remembers those earlier times with disappointment, but she chose to overcome these barriers, as the trailblazer that she is.

> I could look at the condescending smiles and the lack of respect that some people chose to show toward me as a barrier and give up, or I could not let this stop me. I didn't. I cried on numerous occasions, but I learned to pick myself up and continue. I didn't let people's biased perception of me as an African American woman stop me from achieving my goals. I have been very fortunate in my professional life—as you can see on my vita. I could have bowed to those low expectations and quit, but I looked at those barriers as stepping stones to accomplish what I wanted. I had to prove them wrong. It was important to me that I proved myself as a credible person.

After all, Donnya was used to proving her worth to others, beginning as a teacher's child in a segregated public school to a professor at an integrated university she now called her home.

Donnya notes other barriers she faced in the workplace related to salary:

> The women always worked harder than the men but received less pay. The men's excuse for the inequity in salary was that they had a family to support. One of the women instructors was divorced with two children. Didn't she have a family to support?

Another barrier for Donnya was career advancement. Donnya was instrumental in helping one of the professors, who was hired after her, obtain the department chair position. I asked Donnya why she didn't seek the department chair position, and she replied, "Even in the late '90s, this faculty was not ready to be led by an African American woman. They would not accept my leadership."

USE OF MENTORS TO OVERCOME BARRIERS

Many successful educators recognize and acknowledge a strong forum of early support from family, friends, teachers, and mentors. Donnya speaks of barriers as inevitable obstacles: "Regardless of how long you are in a profession, if you are an African American woman, you will always have issues to handle." But Donnya never really felt accepted as an insider in the white institution. These feelings can be described as an outsider-within stance (Collins, 1990). From an insider's perspective, she gained the status of the rank of full professor; however, at times she continued to feel treated as an outsider when it came to being accepted for her academic abilities. For example, she was not included in many of the group research projects being conducted in her department. However, she is quick to point out that later her department chair [one of her mentors] did help her with her writing and included her on several writing projects.

Donnya failed to allow the power of the dominant group to suppress her motivation to achieve her goals and her desire to write; however, being a woman and being black made her a perpetual outsider. This outsider-within position caused Donnya to draw on her early childhood experiences and the memories of her strong matriarchal figures that grounded her in who she was. Donnya spoke often of the significance of her family, friends, and other mentors who served as a viable bridge to her success.

> My mentors were interested in me as an individual. One of my mentors [first department chair] encouraged me to get my doctorate. I took a year's leave from my teaching position to complete my internship. My mentor was instrumental in seeing that I had a teaching job at the institution when I returned.

But there is no doubt that Donnya's greatest mentor was her mother.

> I have been alone throughout my career; I never married and have no children. I have been able to tell my mother anything. My mother was like my sister. When I was teaching in public school, I would go home on the week-

end and we would share experiences, stories, and ideas. When I moved into higher education, my family was my greatest supporter. I left the university to complete my residency while finishing my doctorate. We didn't have a sabbatical. So my family primarily supported me financially for a year while I finished my degree.

There were other mentors, and Donnya speaks fondly of several during the time that she was teaching high school:

In high school my homemaking teacher taught me to cook and sew. She would take me around all over East Texas to model the most current fashion. My high school principal was my mentor. He helped me to believe in myself. I can't believe I once participated successfully in UIL mathematics. I can't work any math today.

Donnya remembers other mentors who were instrumental in helping her obtain her teaching positions. While teaching in a new town, she was fortunate to become acquainted with yet another mentor who became like a godmother and helped her network and become actively involved in the community organizations, such as the Top Ladies of Distinction. She also helped Donnya through the trials of being a young and inexperienced teacher.

Each of Donnya's university department chairs served as mentors. One of her department chairs was a female, but the others were male. The gender of her mentors didn't seem to matter, as she developed wonderful relationships with all of them. They provided encouragement while she was teaching full time and working on her doctorate, and they encouraged her to serve on university-level committees. She was also encouraged to write, and one of her mentors helped her write her first article.

Donnya also spoke of a special mentor who helped her with her leadership skills; this mentor encouraged her to accept the presidency of a local women's association. Later, Donnya served on both state and national boards for this association. Her mentors guided her in developing leadership skills, effective teaching skills, and positive work ethics. These mentors took Donnya under their tutelage and introduced her to other professors within the university as well as to key community leaders. Their endorsement of Donnya led to acceptance by other experienced professors and community leaders that might have taken years to gain on her own.

Donnya has never forgotten her mentors. Her way of showing her gratitude to them is by serving as a mentor to others.

As I write this story to give Donnya's outstanding leadership a voice, I am reminded of what Donnya has done for me as my mentor. I am currently serving as president of one prestigious professional organization on campus and as vice president of a highly respected association in the community. When Donnya steps down from a position on a committee or advisory board, she recommends the instructors she is mentoring to take her place. I am a living witness of the trail that Donnya has blazed and continues to blaze for others today.

DeRamus (1999) writes that "Nobody is born a legend, and most who grow into the role simply rise to the challenges life puts in their paths." Donnya Stephens rose to many challenges life put in her path. She faced both racial and gender biases and a lack of recognition for her academic abilities, and still she rose. She could have "let these stumbling blocks impede my progress, or I could look at them as giving me the energy and motivation to march onward. I chose to march on." Sometimes the trail was dimmed with her tears; often she marched alone, but march on she did, from the segregated classrooms of deep East Texas to a full professorship at a university.

Donnya Stephens continues to teach while on modified retirement. She arrives at work before dawn and remains while many of the full-time professors are long gone. She can be seen on campus conferencing with students, walking down the hallway assisting beginning professors, in the school districts working with student teachers, on campus working with student organizations, and volunteering her services to the university and the community at large. However, the majority of her time is spent mentoring and helping others overcome barriers as they blaze their paths to success. This trailblazer lives her own legacy: "If I can help somebody as I travel along the way, then my living would not be in vain."

> Success is to be measured not so much by the position that one has reached in life as by the obstacles which one has overcome while trying to succeed.
>
> —Booker T. Washington

6

A Portrait of Leadership: Making a Difference

Patsy Hallman by Betty Alford

Life—how great is the living and loving and working. Blessings abound!

—Patsy Hallman

A propensity to action is characteristic of Dr. Patsy Johnson Hallman's life. Dr. Hallman, who currently serves as a professor of education at Stephen F. Austin State University (SFA), is a retired dean of the College of Education and the recipient of many awards. These awards include Phi Delta Kappa Educator of the Year, Nacogdoches Outstanding Educator, the Leadership Award of the Texas Association of the Colleges of Teachers of Education, SFA Distinguished Professor, SFA Woman of the Year by the University Professional Women, and Outstanding Home Economics Teacher in Texas. For 10 years, I had the privilege of working with Dr. Hallman, who is a recognized leader in education. To create a portrait of this outstanding leader, I will share Dr. Hallman's educational experiences, leadership style, personality characteristics, and obstacles and recommendations.

THE EDUCATIONAL EXPERIENCE

Patsy Hallman was born and reared in Miller's Grove, a small town in Northeast Texas. Patsy and her two brothers became disciplined and conscientious under her mother's and father's care. Patsy describes her parents as "smart, hard working, ethical, and nurturing, with high expectations for their children and a commitment to do whatever was necessary for their children to achieve their goals." Though Patsy's mother was a housewife, she had attended teacher's college in Commerce, Texas, and served as a teacher for several years before becoming a mother. She and Patsy's father encouraged Patsy to further her education, beginning with piano lessons as a child and continuing through her graduation as valedictorian of her class, completion of a master's degree, and attainment of her doctoral degree. Patsy comments:

> I guess, looking back, by most standards our family was poor. My father was a house painter and my mother a housewife, but my family was highly respected in the community. I recall commenting to a childhood friend, "Oh, we won't have much for Christmas, either," and the girl replied, "But your mother is a teacher." I could see that, in her eyes, my family held special status, transcending that attained by monetary measures. Education was very important to both of my parents. My brothers and I attended college without acquiring any educational loans. My mother and dad were totally committed to our academic success.

Patsy's interest in becoming a teacher was nurtured by her 1st-grade teacher, Miss Lennon, and another teacher, Mrs. Hatcher, who served as Patsy's teacher for parts of 5 years. Her gifted 1st-grade teacher recognized Patsy's keen intelligence and paired Patsy and another girl, Mary Francis, giving each of them one book after another to complete. When the two girls finished one set of materials, this teacher started them on the next set until each completed both 1st and 2nd grades in 1 year and were promoted to 3rd grade. Patsy and Mary Francis worked together and competed, a catalyst to one another to keep on learning, kindling a love of learning.

Patsy describes Mrs. Hatcher as a lifelong learner who enjoyed participating in summer workshops or courses each year and then incorporating "lessons learned" into classes the next year. Patsy's mother would comment as Patsy came home with woven baskets, dried flowers, or clay pots, "Well, Mrs. Hatcher took another course." This teacher was very traditional, but these enrichments made school fun. Patsy first continued her path of learning by acquiring her teaching certification and master's degree in home economics. She married and had two children before moving to Nacogdoches, Texas, where her husband had accepted a position as professor in the Department of Guidance and Counseling. Patsy had taught high school home economics prior to coming to Nacogdoches and was recruited to teach part time for Nacogdoches High School.

Soon, the Department of Home Economics at Stephen F. Austin State University asked if Patsy would teach for them. Patsy recalls,

> I'm thinking of the path toward work in higher education that I was almost pushed into by my mother and major professor via a master's degree program, and then the highly unlikely way in which I was given my first position in college teaching—mainly because someone did not report to work, and I was the only one with the essential qualifications of a master's degree. My first college teaching contract was for one semester only, with assurances that local policy wouldn't allow me to have another contract. Of course, the reality is that my career at the university has been one semester plus 35 years—from the lowest paid professor on campus to a dean. . . . While we believe (and we work accordingly) that we must plan, set goals, and work to achieve them, in reality, it is the totally unexpected and unplanned for events that often most dramatically affect our lives.

To attain a doctoral degree, a requirement for continued university teaching, Patsy drove to Denton, Texas, for classes. Each summer, she would "load the children" in the car and drive the 5 hours to Texas Women's University in North Texas to complete coursework. She finished her PhD in home economics with a specialization in management and taught in the Department of Home Economics for 22 years. Then, in 1992, she became associate dean for the College of Education. Patsy credits Dean Tom Franks for selecting her as associate dean and then giving her the freedom to make decisions and to work for productivity in educational programs. Upon Dean Frank's retirement, Patsy became interim dean and then the dean of the College of Education. Patsy's scholarly activities have included coauthoring five textbooks as well as writing two biographies, a book for successful teenagers, and many articles and proposals for educational grants.

LEADERSHIP STYLE

Patsy Hallman's leadership style is characterized by collaboration, action orientation, personal integrity, work patterns and balance, and mentoring experiences. Patsy is an action-oriented woman who is truly making a difference and wasting no time in doing so. Through her work, her knowledge of ability and personnel are clearly evident in a leadership style of making things happen in a collaborative environment characterized by openness and trust. While Dr. Hallman was associate dean at SFA, the Center for Professional Development and Technology, which she served as director and primary proposal author, was funded for $1,317,000 for 3 years. This grant provided funding for restructuring teacher and administrator education to include increased field experiences, provision of technology for the university and partner schools, establishment of a recruitment program for minority students, and implementation of a staff development plan for the College of Education and five partner school districts. The grant from the Texas Education Agency was combined with a grant from Southwestern Bell to equip the College of Education for distance learning and to provide training in its use. To coordinate these grants, Patsy established six action teams of university and school district educators who served as advisory groups for the various components of the grant.

Collaboration

A master at summarizing the main points that are made and focusing a discussion, Patsy is often called on to provide a synopsis of a meeting and key issues yet to be discussed. Patsy's talent in the facilitation of meetings was recognized at State Directors of Centers for Professional Development and Technology meetings, where she frequently serves as the leader of collaborative working groups. Though recognized for keeping a meeting focused and productive, Patsy also is recognized as a master at collaboration. Her trust in the collaborative process is clearly illustrated by her willingness to support the collaborative decision even when the ideas that are reached differed from her first recommendation.

Action Orientation

Another characteristic of Patsy's leadership style is the ability to move ideas to action, setting a tone of proactiveness and preparedness by her actions. For example, when a report was due to the state for the grant's operation, she would begin work on it immediately upon receiving the request and finish it far in advance of the due date. A master at delegation, she would divide tasks among many persons and provide follow-up. Ownership in the process was fostered by the continual delegation of responsibilities, though once responsibilities were delegated, great freedom and latitude were given to the person for design of the task. When Patsy delegated a responsibility, she assumed the person would do it well. A timeline was established, and she would follow up on the timeline, but she always allowed individual creativity and initiative in completing the work. In terms of leadership style, her eye is always on the horizon even as she is working diligently in the present. A keeper of the vision, Patsy keeps the vision alive through ongoing communication processes.

Personal Integrity

An important characteristic of Patsy's leadership style is her personal integrity. Patsy always works diligently herself even as responsibilities are delegated, ever modeling her belief in the importance of the educational restructuring effort to better prepare teachers to meet 21st-century needs. Patsy demonstrates her belief that teacher and administrator preparation should be restructured to include a greater field-based component, with strategies to increase technological skills, through her positive actions to achieve this goal. Her leadership style received recognition by invitations to present information about the teacher education restructured program at state and national conferences.

WORK PATTERNS AND BALANCE

Keeping a nonstop pace throughout the day is characteristic of Patsy's work. A master at organization, timelines, and quick thinking, Patsy is very focused, with a well-designed sequence noticeable in her work. If she is preparing a major report, the total office staff becomes focused on this task. Work is divided neatly in stacks as each section is completed. The work is not done to the exclusion of other office responsibilities, which are numerous, but the primary focus is very clear. Fast, thorough, and conscientious, the work moves quickly until the finished product begins to emerge. The ability to focus intently on a project, complete it, and move on to the next challenge is characteristic of the pattern of Patsy Hallman's work.

However, in spite of the enormous number of projects completed, Patsy is also a master at separating home and work and achieving balance in her life. Although she works at an extremely fast pace, at 5:00 P.M. she leaves for the day and generally takes no work home. She believes in the importance of family time and has often said to others, "Don't you need to go spend time with your family?"

Over 10 years ago, Patsy and her first husband divorced; a few years later, she married Leon Hallman, who currently serves as Director of International Studies at SFA. When she remarried, two households were combined, resulting in five teenagers in the home. Currently, all have graduated and are self-supporting. However, Patsy continues her practice of "leaving work at work" as much as possible, saving time for a quality relationship with her family and volunteer work with her church. Pausing to consider the impact of her marriage to Leon on her career, Patsy expresses that her professional life has been strengthened by the quality of her relationship with him. "Sharing life with a loving and compatible partner is enriching and nurturing."

Patsy believes strongly that it is important to have quality family time, and she tries not to let work infringe on this. In addition, she entertains and maintains friendships away from work. An active member of the Methodist church, she and her husband assume leadership roles on church councils and in teaching Sunday school classes. Patsy recalls an admonition of her mother that she has lived by: "When someone asks you to do something for your community, you do it." Since time is of the essence in achieving her professional goals while maintaining her family life during evenings at home, when traveling to meetings, Patsy always takes a PowerBook and briefcase of work and uses every spare minute to get tasks accomplished. However, though she makes every minute count, Patsy balances work, home life, and spiritual life and achieves the joy of helping. She states succinctly:

God, who created us, must surely want us to enjoy the life He has given. When I see happiness in a child's face, when I sense a prayer answered, when I sit by my fire on a cold winter day, relaxing with a good book, when I finish a worthy task . . . at these times, I know the joy of just being.

Mentoring Experiences

Patsy has served as a mentor to several people. Two students lived in her home while completing their master's degrees, and through her encouragement, one of the students completed her doctoral degree. For the three administrative assistants who worked in her office, one as secretary, one as certification officer, and one as student teaching administrator, Patsy allowed each flexibility in completing coursework toward their undergraduate degrees while working in the office. She wanted them to succeed, so she provided the flexible work schedule to make this happen.

I know the power of her mentorship through her role in my career. As assistant director of the Center of Professional Development and Technology, I was always included in state, regional, and local meetings in addition to serving as a copresenter in workshop settings. Always, I felt a valuable part of the team. When my schedule with work presented conflicts as I was completing my doctoral degree, she merely said, "We want to help you get the degree. Someone did this for me." As my first year at Stephen F. Austin State University progressed in my work as an assistant director for a grant, Patsy said, "We want you to start teaching some classes," encouraging my transition to college teaching, in addition to my grant responsibilities. Knowing that the grant would end in a year, she provided me with opportunities as she opened doors for my future. Patsy embodies the characteristics of a true mentor to me and to many, providing unconditional positive regard, opening doors, providing opportunities for growth, and serving as a friend.

PERSONALITY CHARACTERISTICS

Humble

Humble, energetic, and resourceful are characteristics to describe Patsy's personality. On one trip to a meeting, I especially recall riding in a van with educators from across the nation as we traveled from the airport to the hotel. Each person seemed to be trying to surpass the other as he or she told of places visited and work accomplished. As I listened to their boasting, I thought, in contrast, that in working with Patsy for a year and a half, I learned of her travels only incidentally, though she has traveled extensively, to China, Japan, Alaska, Mexico, Europe, throughout the U.S. mainland, and Nova Scotia, Canada. Her experiences far surpassed those who were riding in the van, yet she never alluded to her travels and accomplishments.

Energetic

Patsy Hallman is also extremely energetic, walking every morning or evening to maintain her small size and good health, energetically walking the stairs in the four-story Department of Education building and avoiding the elevator. Her energy seems without bound. She tells a story of her mother's sister that illustrates, in part, a source of her energy:

> When my 83-year-old aunt helped my sister-in-law in the race for State School Board member, she arrived at the office one morning and told her nephew, "Let's go put some signs in the yards in neighborhoods." This was at 8:00 A.M. At 4:30 P.M., the nephew said, "Aunt Faye, could we please stop now?"

This 83-year-old lady was still "going strong" and could have easily worked until dark. This same energy is exemplified by Patsy.

Resourceful

Patsy is resourceful. In fact, a twinkle appears in her eye as she illustrates just how resourceful she can be with the following anecdote:

> A few years ago, I was teaching in the off-campus program at a site over an hour away from home. I had gone home to work on a book that I was writing. Always time conscious, I was working up to the very last minute when the professor who was traveling with me to the site arrived. I jumped up, dashed out the door, and hopped in my car for the drive. I thought I had left a pair of shoes in the car.
>
> When I got closer to the site, I began looking for my shoes. I had a habit of kicking my shoes off under the seat and thought they were there. However, I soon realized I had left them at home. I turned to my rider and proposed a plan. "We'll go in a store quickly. You can divert the salesclerk, and maybe she won't notice I have no shoes on as I enter, and I'll buy some shoes."

If the salesclerk did notice, I doubt it even fazed the impeccably dressed, petite woman who purchased a pair of shoes quickly and dashed out the door. Dr. Hallman and I have laughed together over this story, a story that encapsulates her personal characteristics of being focused, purposeful, energetic, resourceful, undaunted, and time conscious. These are but some of the characteristics that describe Patsy Hallman. Sincerity, warmth, caring, and intelligence are other descriptors I would list.

OBSTACLES AND RECOMMENDATIONS

Being Place-Bound

Patsy's accomplishments have not all come easily. Her story is no exception to obstacles. Early in her career at the university level, she served as an administrative intern in the office of the vice president for academic affairs, a step to immediate advancement. However, because of family obligations, Patsy chose to be "place-bound" and stay at the university where she had done the internship rather than to immediately pursue an opening in educational leadership, and there were no openings at her current university. Though Patsy was instrumental to the university's success, she chose to remain teaching for 22 years before moving into the field of administration. In addition, she served as interim dean for 2 years rather than apply at another university. Having accomplished so much, Patsy has no regrets, but she acknowledges that not being willing to move may have delayed her progression to the position of dean.

Limited Acceptance of Women as Leaders

Even though Patsy is an energetic woman and very capable in her professional expertise, not all were ready to accept a woman as dean, another obstacle that she had to overcome. With her strong faith and a strong network of family and friends, obstacles never became a source of complaint. Instead, they were simply realities that she would take action to overcome, not realities that sealed her fate. Her life serves as reinforcement to other women to pursue their dreams and to take action, recognizing that the rewards will come along the way. Patsy's advice to other women is, "Always remember to take advantage of opportunities whenever they come—whether you have prompted their appearance by your own actions or whether they are totally unexpected."

> Whatever I think is right for me to do, I do. I do the things that I believe ought to be done. And when I make up my mind to do a thing, I act.
>
> —Theodore Roosevelt

7

Artful Leadership Outside the Box

Candace Newland by Carolyn Carr

I see every person I become involved with as a potential teacher, whether they are a staff member, a child, or a community member. One of my greatest gifts is the ability to recognize opportunity in relationships.

—Candace Newland

Memories of childhood school days abound for Candace Newland as she thinks back about her life as an educator. She grew up in a family of educators. Her father taught high school biology, coached, and had been an assistant principal and high school principal. Her mother taught kindergarten for many years. Even as a child, Candace would watch out for other children who had problems or for whom life posed difficult challenges in their school, families, or neighborhood. She loved other children and had a gift for helping them. For example, when she was only 10, she became an interpreter for Mickey, a 4-year-old boy who had been adopted. He had a private language his parents couldn't understand, but it was perfectly clear to Candace. Naturally, and to their surprise and delight, she taught his parents how to understand Mickey. The life of the family was changed. Today, with her extensive experience as an educator, Candace thinks Mickey was probably autistic. But back then, he was just a child she cared about and could help. She has never wavered from those early instincts, and recognition of her extraordinary skills and mastery of the art of leadership brought her honor as the National Elementary Distinguished Principal for the state of Oregon in 1998.

EARLY SCHOOL MEMORIES

A variety of things come quickly to mind as Candace thinks back to her own early school days. She laughs as she remembers in elementary school having to hold out her hands every morning so that her teachers could check to see that the students' fingernails were clean. For those who failed the test, names went up on the blackboard.

Candace remembers loving to read and reading everything she could for hours at a time. But she also remembers being very involved physically, winning handball tournaments and playing chase games. She was a student body officer at the elementary level. She learned Spanish in talented and gifted classes and participated in elementary school choir, wearing costumes and performing dances from all over the world.

One incident from the 4th grade is still particularly vivid. One day, she and her best friend got the giggles. Their teacher told them to stop laughing and not to speak again. Of course, they burst into laughter again. The teacher pulled Candace up in front of everyone and actually spanked her with a wooden board with holes in it. As she recalls, he

> told me to bend over, touch my toes, and spanked me four times on my bottom. I was extremely humiliated. It took me about 45 minutes to walk home because I was sobbing so. My parents had never spanked me in my life. They never yelled at me because I was by and large very well disciplined. But this particular teacher had been one of my dad's favorite athletes in high school, and I thought I had it made in the shade. The huge irony about it is that later, years later, when I was 56 years old, he came in as substitute custodian for my own school. He had been a teacher, principal, and then one of those "Eveready batteries" that just keep running. He was a substitute custodian and introduced himself. I asked him if he had ever taught mathematics at the elementary level, and he said he had. I said, "I remember when you spanked me, 46 years ago in front of the class." He asked if it had traumatized me, and I replied, "Would I be talking about it 46 years later if it hadn't?" He felt horrible. I was glad.

Laughing at this point, Candace recalls how very ironic the whole incident had been because she was an excellent student, very well behaved and responsible. It had been an unfortunate incident when she had gotten the giggles, and an adult had felt compelled to exert his power and make an example of a child's natural behavior.

Another memory focused on mathematics in junior high. She had a fabulous teacher who set up problems for the students to solve each week. He made mathematics exciting by using the precursor of a math problem-solving model, which was to be known nationally as Lane County Math Problem Solving. Candace was converted to a math wizard during her junior high years because of this teacher's influence. Years later she went back to university to be trained in the model and brought it back to her district. This same teacher worked with her again and told her that the year he taught her in 7th-grade math class was his first year teaching. She counts him as one of the most outstanding teachers she ever had in her life.

An achiever in athletics as well as in academics, in junior high school Candace could outleap all the boys in the long jump, and her time in the 800 meters was faster than most high school girls run today. Athletics ran in her family. Dad was a track coach, and brother Bob was a wide receiver for the New Orleans Saints in the National Football League. She always had a dream of receiving a standing ovation like Bob—and finally got one from her students when she retired.

Candace remembers her sister, 2 years older, giving her advice and saying it was going to be really hard on Candace when she went to high school, where her dad was the vice principal. When Candace naively asked why, her wise older sister told her she wouldn't be able to get away with anything. And further, she couldn't get involved in any difficulties. Candace looked at her curiously and asked, "What would you want to do that you wouldn't want dad to know about?" That was the kind of kid she remembers being: smart, athletic, and a little goody two-shoes!

EDUCATIONAL BACKGROUND

When Candace first went to the University of Oregon as a freshman, her ambition was to be an international lawyer. She had an intense interest in developing nations in Africa and communism in Russia. She loved international relations. But life intervened in her early plans when she married and had a child. Candace dropped out of school partly because of her marriage, but another important contributing factor at the time was her investment in the Vietnam War. She remembers a very confusing time in America. Her senior class president died in Vietnam, as did the first boy she ever dated. She did not support the war, and it was a horribly tumultuous time in her own mind because her own political science department was polarized between supporters and protesters of the war. Candace had a hard time reading newspapers, watching television, and balancing what people said about the war with what she knew was happening there. She was involved in marches and went to events protesting the war, but was never arrested. It was time for her to say she did not want to be in school at that time; it was her way of dropping out temporarily.

For a while Candace worked for a stock brokerage. It was completely different from anything she had ever done. She felt like a black sheep in her family because her sister went straight through college, and her younger brother was also in college at the time. Working in business was contrary to everything the children had been programmed to do, but it was what she needed to do at that time. In retrospect, working in the brokerage and not making any money was a good experience because one day she woke up and said, "Oh, I'm just the fingers for someone else's brains. I don't want to do this. I really want to go back and be more in charge of things, and my own life, and get a better salary. I need to go back to school."

Candace enrolled in Oregon State University and went directly into elementary education to become a teacher. She realized that she wanted to know more about nurturing her own child. She wanted to be a better parent and raise her daughter well, and also work with other children in a school. Her thinking and her academic focus changed. Part of her didn't want a degree in education because she thought the coursework was too easy, not challenging enough for her broad and deep interests. Yet she realized she had two different sides, each poles apart: strongly intellectual and international interests along with a deeply nurturing and caring concern for children.

LEADERSHIP STYLE EMERGES

Candace became a teacher and worked in curriculum for about 11 years. Part of her inspiration for change was that she did not see schools being run the way she thought they should be run. So she went to Portland State University and earned her basic administrative credential. As Candace observed administrators, she began to consider this work for herself. She recalls observing principals who played favorites with the staff, creating groups of haves and have-nots. Some teachers had more access to time, attention, and material resources. She disliked the divisiveness of that: making people compete for resources and creating an environment filled with little trust or love or collaboration. She told herself that one of the ways she could be brought into school leadership was by someone recognizing her strengths and talents and then mentoring her as a "chosen one." Another way was by seeing what didn't exist and dreaming of an environment that was more healthful and would produce better results for teaching and learning. Candace was of the latter persuasion. She began dreaming of her ideal school.

It took only 2 years to get her first administrative job, a comparatively short time considering she had known other candidates who waited 10 years before they were selected. She could not imagine having that kind of patient endurance herself. Once hired, Candace worked in the same district for 26 years.

Understanding the Change Process

Candace joined a professional women's group early in her administrative career, and it was there that she gained important personal insights. She realized she initially tended to make changes too quickly because of her own ability to grasp information rapidly and then seek out ways of experimenting and doing things in new ways. Initially she assumed everyone behaved the same way, not realizing that adults had different levels of readiness for change, different levels of intelligence, and different perceptions of school reform. One of the retired women in her group advised Candace to consider her staff as students in her classroom and help them learn about changes at their own rates and in their own ways. That gave her a different way of approaching the staff, and she could start looking at them as individuals, their years of experience, levels of conservatism or progressivism, and emotional needs. This realization freed her to become an effective leader.

Mentoring Help

Several other female supervisors mentored Candace as a principal. They constantly encouraged her and helped her read the pulse of different situations she faced. She could bring any issue to them and know it would not be judged but treated professionally. The most helpful mentors she recalls were African American women. They were never angry with her, but were reasonable, listened with care, and then brought in their own wisdom about what to do. Her mentors gave her increased ability to express herself, problem-solved with her, encouraged her intellect, and trusted her emotions and intuition. Candace recalls their mentoring as an awesome experience, full of learning, growth, and confidence building for her.

STYLE INTO SUBSTANCE: AN ARTS MAGNET SCHOOL

Candace was inspired as a young child by music and art and movement. Connecting these with mathematics and literacy made her feel so thrilled about herself as a learner.

The Vision

In her fifth year as a school principal, the day came when Candace's interests came together in a vision of what school could be, a vision that was to shape her career. She began to dream about what an ideal school would look like and about all she had learned in educational research about best practices. Her dream became a vision of an arts magnet school. She thought about her own two daughters and how they had very creative styles like her own. She thought how wonderful it would have been if they had been able to go to a school like she was envisioning. She started writing 6 hours a day—at different times, even in the middle of the night. The only time she didn't write was during work time, but she wrote continually for 6 weeks.

An Uneasy Alliance

Candace developed a conceptual plan for an arts magnet. She found an ally in her boss, who had been the first African American woman visual arts teacher in South Carolina. They worked and communicated with each other until the plan took shape, and then they printed it and presented it to the superintendent. He also was thrilled and put Candace in touch with the curriculum department in the district, and they began collaboration as well. At this level, Candace was initiated into the intricacies of central office politics and professional rivalries, for it was highly unusual for a principal to be given access in such a formidable way to creation of an important innovation. The superintendent's support made the uneasy alliance work, but it was very awkward. Candace felt constantly put down and underutilized, but she learned to persevere. The uneasy team visited nationally prominent arts magnet school sites that had received distinguished school awards. They gathered material from these schools that helped immensely in determining what would be done in Portland. Obstacles abounded in actually beginning the school, but Candace would not give up her vision. With the help of federal grants and an excited and supportive superintendent, Buckman Elementary became her school—and the future lay open before her.

Building Trust

Change was rapid and filled with detours. Candace's mother died, and within 5 days Candace held her first staff meeting with a faculty totally unaware of both the shift in principals and the change from a traditional school to an arts magnet school. In her inimitable style, however, Candace started developing relationships and showing the faculty and community how much of what they were already doing fit in with what they were going to do in an arts magnet school. She gradually built their trust, which was essential considering the condition of the school.

By 1989 enrollment at Buckman had dropped from 520 students to 300. A third of the classrooms were empty. The building was run down and in need of maintenance and paint. In the summer of 1989, Candace became the fifth principal in 5 years. There was a 50% poverty rate and a huge transient student rate. Of the 63 elementary schools in the district, Buckman was ranked as one of the 13 lowest. For every child who came in, one left.

Achieving a High Standard

By 1992 the school was a very different place. Candace had resurrected a failing neighborhood school and transformed it into one of the best magnets in the entire school district. Remodeled physically and in its spirit, the school became a model of progressive education. Over the 9 years Candace was there, Buckman became one of the highest achieving elementary schools in the district. Bright kids who were divergent thinkers and wanted a more exciting nontraditional curriculum were attracted to the school. Students came back to Buckman from private schools. Even realtors came in and said the school had transformed the neighborhood; now people wanted to buy there. There were English language learners in the school—20 different languages were spoken by 100 out of 500—a high special education population, and by the end of the program, one of the highest talented and gifted populations in the district. It was a rich mixture. One parent attributed all this to Candace:

> Her commitment to arts education is legendary. She understands as few administrators do that academics alone can't adequately prepare children for the conundrums of the new millennium. She knows the arts play a unique role in educating the whole child and that the skills students develop practicing the arts—flexibility, intuition, creativity, discipline, persistence, and the ability to work collaboratively—will be prized personally, socially, and in the 21st-century workplace.

Dealing with Conflict

Such an enormous transition did not happen overnight; it took 9 years of hard work. Conflict, controversy, and stress surrounded Candace's every attempt to bring about the changes that occurred. By nature, Candace is very much a peacemaker rather than an antagonistic or confrontational person. To constantly assert herself without being confrontational or unpleasant was a challenging journey for her. She had to make sure her supervisors were apprised of what the school was doing so that it had their support. Sometimes the superintendent had to actually square off with somebody who was opposing the school. Candace was conscious of the constant need to build support and advocacy for the program, to work with people in a parent community who would be strong advocates, and to build a staff that really cared about and respected each other, who could stand for and value what the school was doing. One supporter asserts that Candace's masterful ability to somehow, some way, find resources and energy to keep Buckman thriving is legendary among parents, staff, and community members. She knows how to inspire and to delegate.

For example, at one point early on, Candace was told the school would lose 10% of its funds and a number of staff. She describes that year as a horrible financial one for the district. The way she was trained in college to discuss budget reductions was to bring in the local school committee, site council, and staff and talk about what they valued and wanted to keep. But the unions didn't want the staff thinking and talking about those things because, after all, they might stand in judgment about one of their colleagues, and that might be against the collective bargaining agreement.

In that instance, Candace remembers, she was always thinking how she could do a better job with this principalship and school, in terms of being a steward, an ancestor. So she called in her nine most trusted parents, who included the head of the School Foundation, the head of judicial fitness review for the state, and the head of the city planning commission. The group came from different backgrounds, many legal, but they were community organizers who knew more about the community and working with each other than Candace did. She did not want to do the traditional three or four meetings. But she had no idea how to walk through this; she was terrified of what had to be done and felt it was all on her shoulders. She needed information to make the best decision—which would be unpopular, and people would no doubt be angry. Whichever way she went, people would feel ill will toward her. She needed more involvement and expertise than she herself could muster.

Team Building

The team developed a 6-week timeline of 10 meetings, balanced between day, evening, and afternoon so as many people as possible could communicate. The meetings involved site council, staff, and community—all helped map out a strategy, and they even took over many of the meetings and tasks. At the beginning of each meeting, people would talk about what they valued. What kinds of things could they not do without? Meetings always started in this wonderful uplifting way. Candace remembers having a heavy heart dragging her down so that she could hardly walk into those sessions. Yet this spirit they brought with them, and this way to look at the staff's thinking and start graphing what they found, was incredible. She was able to take all the data and summarize it and then make decisions on what to keep and not keep. Of course it was hellish in terms of the aftermath because they lost staff and some programs. Some people threw tantrums and protested, but there was always that ability to think outside the box and ask what was the most important thing for the kids. Because the team involved the community, they were important players in terms of leadership as well as participation.

During that time, one parent said that anyone could go to Candace with an idea and she would listen to them and then ask them questions about how to do this, what would it take, what kind of support did they need—and always run it by the staff, too. As a result of those parents who came in, a rich community formed and the synergy just expanded what the school could do for children. Clearly, Candace was known for the honest recognition of her limitations and her eager willingness to bring in people to help instead of trying to be all things to all people. She was humble enough to admit something was not her area of expertise and sought those who could be *her* teachers.

One of the nomination letters for the Distinguished Principal Award asserts:

> Candace has a clear vision, is tireless in executing it, and she is extraordinarily effective in getting results. Teachers, parents, community leaders—even those that start out skeptical—come away believing in her vision and wanting to help. She builds community within and without the school's walls. She is unafraid to ask for help, or set high goals and expectations.

A TYPICAL DAY FOR CANDACE

As a principal, Candace routinely began her day by 4:30 A.M. with exercise; she was well aware that once the day began at school she would not have a whole lot of control over her time. She had to be responsive to whatever needed to be done. Sometimes she did not get home until after 10:00 P.M., but mostly she would get home by 6:30. Days were very long, and the longer she worked in that kind of situation, the harder it became physically because the endurance, tenacity, and resilience the work required were overwhelming.

Authentic Presence

Generally, Candace arrived at school by 7:15 A.M. Her day began with greeting children and then cruising around the building classrooms once things got started well. She always checked in with any people having special events in their lives—physical tests, birthdays, or challenges with students or parents. After making sure everyone was ready for the day, Candace spent her days working with teachers, substitutes, parents, and students. It was not unusual to see her stopping in the hall to talk with a student, or popping into a classroom to check on a student with a special need. Candace was genuinely joyful in the presence of student creators, communicating a sense of appreciation—even awe—at what they were exploring or producing. Her consistent acknowledgment and validation of people's strengths, talents, and contributions had an exhilarating effect on them.

In her last year as principal she spent time working with teacher teams at all grade levels, writing student goals in language that could be shared with students and parents. She was always watching out for those people who, if given a little more, could bring the environment into more harmony. She tried to be like a coach in as many ways as she could to keep everyone thinking about creating the best environment for teaching and learning.

Authentic Concern for Democratic Schooling

Candace's last school was very affluent, so one of her primary focuses was the fact that she loved cultural diversity, loved having all of society together, and loved all that about public schools. In that school was a group of people who believed that affluence equaled influence and that children who were disenfranchised, who were poor, weren't as important. Undaunted, Candace introduced Ruby Payne's framework for working with children of poverty and talked about what it is like to have a parent in prison or not have a medical card, or what it is like if you came into a classroom and a great number of students were going to Europe, Africa, or Asia over the holiday, and you weren't even sure you were going to have a holiday celebration, much less a birthday party.

Candace tried to equalize the playing field as much as possible, such as by helping the community understand that it wasn't okay to have afternoon classes for the wealthy students only, with a $150 charge, when everyone else would like to have after-school activities as well. She worked with a number of concepts very contrary to the fundamental values that some of the key parent leaders held. Some became quite angry and complained to her boss. The majority felt good about what she was doing, but there were always those who weren't fully democratized and didn't know how to work in an honest and careful and supportive way in a school. Candace spent her days on much more substantive issues than buses, books, and budgets.

PERSONAL LIFE CHALLENGES

For Candace, family is a huge issue. Her family has had a clear impact on her career. They were definite assets to her work and in understanding what was needed. By being a parent, she learned important lessons that she wouldn't have known about school or education or teachers or learning without having gone through it with her own children.

As an example, Candace relates a story about when her older daughter, always a high achiever and involved with accelerated classes, encountered an immovable force in her senior honors English teacher. She was senior class president and was taking three college credit classes and participating on the track team, often coming home from track meets and working until midnight on homework. As an educator, Candace knew how the high school was supposed to work together to ensure no one subject unreasonably dominated a student's workload. This particular teacher demanded students read a whole novel per week, a loftier standard than any other teacher, and the load was overwhelming her daughter. Candace worked her way from the unresponsive teacher up to the principal, trying to change her daughter's class. Candace cites this as an example of how if she hadn't been a parent and seen it personally, she might not have known the importance of the tenet that teachers work together and figure out how to collaborate effectively and appropriately on homework expectations.

Another example occurred with her other daughter, who was 5 years younger and rebellious at the time. She didn't want to do what everyone else wanted her to do. She had slacked off in her work in the 4th grade and wasn't turning in her assignments. The teacher made no contact with Candace, who learned that her daughter was doing miserably when she went in for the 9-week parent-teacher conference. The teacher had never called or sent notice. For Candace this was one of the greatest examples of the need for careful monitoring of work in terms of daily planners/weekly planners and communication. As Candace recalls the story,

> I am a kind, respectful person, but I was really outraged that 9 weeks of time had gone by and I wasn't apprised that there was a problem. There are all sorts of different things that occur to kids in school that help you see what best practices are, what humane treatment is, what is respectful. There is great humility in being a parent and feeling how a teacher talks to you about your child and makes judgments. This is always such an equalizer, like a mirror to see what I needed to do as school leader through what was happening with my own children.

Candace acknowledges doing a better job of balancing work and home at the beginning of her career. Having a spouse to support her, to help with the children, economically and otherwise, to talk to was very important. As her two daughters grew older and left home, she let her work take more and more of her life; soon her personal life felt very small compared to her professional life. She is not sure how much of this was choice and how much was by demand. As she observes professional colleagues, she does not see very many successful school administrators having much of a personal life, as much as they try. Often in situations like her own, one partner becomes so successful that it becomes difficult for the mate to accept and be an encourager on an equal level, and the marriage stumbles, as hers did 3 years ago. Being alone can be lonely, but Candace has always worked hard to stay physically fit, eat right, and make sure she could support her health through the horrific emotional and mental challenges of administration work. She always made time for friends and family. She loved movies and made time for personal reading, but often those pleasures, in terms of balance, wouldn't come for her until the weekends. Often one of those weekend days was also spent working, preparing for the next week.

PROFESSIONAL BARRIERS

When Candace was working on her administrative credential, the head of the administration program called her into his office and talked to her, saying he wanted her to be very careful because he could see she had a very liberal mind that was concerned deeply with educational reform. He was afraid that if she were to share all her complex thinking with colleagues she would never be accepted by them. The professor forewarned her to be more quiet rather than noisy in the beginning of her career. He also warned her to change her dress from the bright, colorful designer dresses she favored to a more conservative fashion statement. It was a more conservative time in the 1970s, and he told her to go out and look at what other administrators, predominantly male, were wearing. She did so, and sure enough she saw them in black, white, and shades of gray. The feminist part of Candace was very strong at the time and, irritated, she went to see her dad that weekend to check the professor's advice. Her dad agreed with the professor, telling his reluctant daughter that as an "out-of-the-box thinker," she would encounter many conservative people in educational administration who would resent her and think her too radical to fit in. They would figure out ways to sabotage her. He advised her to be careful not to share all her progressive ideas and, furthermore, to buy conservative suits as the price of fitting into "the club." Over time she could become more of her own person. He sagely told her she did not have to lose who she was just because she was more quiet at the beginning of her career. She did not have to lose who she was because she *looked like them*.

The stereotype that to be a good administrator one needed to act like a man was very strong in the early days of Candace's career. One needed to be hard-nosed, not soft; aggressive, not collaborative. To be gentle, firm, and hold your ground, yet compromise if needed, was not acceptable behavior. Admitting mistakes was seen as a liability. Today, Candace sees many of these traits inverted among the more effective principals. For them the change has come only with much time, practice, experience, and feedback from supervisors, colleagues, staff, and community. Candace herself has grown and developed internal confidence to judge herself by her own internal standards, helped, she admits, by some less than successful experiences when she was humbled by disagreements and grievances. She has learned that she must keep growing and understand she will never be beloved by everyone.

LEADERSHIP SKILLS THAT HAVE SERVED HER WELL

When asked about her most effective leadership skills, Candace explains without hesitation that at her core is a very caring, loving heart that reaches out to every person with whom she works and every person she meets. She sees every person she becomes involved with as a potential teacher, whether he or she is a staff member, a child, or a community member. One of her greatest gifts is the ability to recognize opportunity in relationships. Candace is very honest and does not play games with people; she admits when she has made an error in judgment or procedure. But she is also very careful and knows the law well so that she can protect herself and her people from getting hurt by any legal action. She avoids becoming involved in collusion against other people and tries to minimize adversarial relationships. Candace always tries to figure out how everyone can be a winner, so a teacher feels good about his or her work; a child is guided into the most productive citizen and learner he or she can be; and parents feel they have been listened to. Perhaps her greatest skill is the ability to have fun and celebrate life and learning.

Today in her new position as the director of the Center for Student Success at Portland State University, Candace finds herself learning a whole new set of leadership skills as she begins the challenge of linking school districts and their needs with the university resources available to them in an era of school reform. She recognizes that in her practitioner background she worked hard and was recognized for that work, but now she must prepare herself to see school reform needs at a more generalized level across districts. She sees herself as an educator and teacher who must develop new skills in giving back to the community. Developing a structure and plan for the new center and blazing a path in order to open opportunities for increasing the breadth and depth of knowledge in the university with school districts is a whole new challenge for her.

ADVICE FOR ASPIRING WOMEN LEADERS

After 32 years as an educator, Candace is still "thinking outside the box." She also wears bright and stylish clothes! As she retired from her principalship career she began looking forward to continued work in education, expanding her knowledge and leadership into a broader area than a single school or district. She loves to write and is interested in developing those skills and sharing them with the wider educational community. She enjoys traveling, learning from others, and working collaboratively with

8

The Quest for Excellence

Bette Davis by Faye Hicks-Townes

But anyway, I just want you to know that whatever achievements people think I have, I owe.

—Bette Davis

Bette Davis, a petite African American woman, has taught English and composition for over 35 years. The oldest of four sisters, Bette "played the grown-up with them, helping my mother, especially after our father died, leaving her a widow at 28 years old." She taught high school for 27 years, junior college for 2 years, and is currently in her eighth year of teaching at the college level in her home state of Mississippi. A recipient of two Spencer Foundation grants, Bette has consistently honed her skills in teaching and writing. Most recently honored as humanities teacher of the year at William Carey College, where she works today, Bette has also been selected as Teacher of the Year at Jones Junior College, where she was an English instructor, and for the Hattiesburg School District, where she taught high school English.

A THIRST FOR KNOWLEDGE

Since childhood, Bette has loved reading and writing. She recounts early memories:

> I also read at home. By the time I was 9, I could walk the mile to our little "branch" of the town's public library. It took up about four shelves in a corner of a room in our community center. I can't remember the books I checked out of the library then, but I know some of them contained poetry by Phillis Wheatley and Paul Laurence Dunbar.

Bette began her formal education in Mississippi's public segregated school system. Her first 9 years of school were spent at Eureka Junior High School. As a child, she had dreams and ambitions that were not necessarily nurtured by a society segregated along racial lines.

> When I was a child I liked to play around with writing and . . . I didn't even consider teaching. You could not have told me. But you know what, I had pipe dreams when I was a child. Because I remember now, my earliest career dream was to be a stenographer. Now where was I going to do that in Mississippi? But I'll tell you I graduated from that dream to another one. I wanted to be a journalist. So . . . it was all writing connected. I wanted to be a journalist. And I don't even think I knew what journalism entailed. All I knew was that I wanted to write for a newspaper, or maybe even for a magazine. As poor as I grew up, I had no clue where I was going to study journalism because they certainly didn't offer it at Alcorn or Jackson State. And I did not know where I was going to practice journalism. Because I certainly could not have worked for the Hattiesburg *American* in the 1960s. You know what I mean?

Bette went on to graduate from Rowan High School with honors. A couple of weeks later she left home to attend Alcorn A&M College, a predominantly black institution in Mississippi. She attended Alcorn for 3 years before she had to leave to work full time. When she returned to college "we could go to USM," so Bette completed her undergraduate degree at the University of Southern Mississippi. The move from predominantly black Alcorn to predominantly white USM was quite a change.

> Yes indeed it was a big change. . . . I lived at home while I was at USM, and I did not get into the socialization part of school as I had at Alcorn. But

. . . of course, . . . quite frankly, I did not feel as comfortable. It was my first integrated situation, period, school or otherwise.

Although Bette faced some challenges in this new environment, she persevered.

I did okay. I did fine in the class, but I really was kind of out of the loop. Even when they were having class conversations on the literature, a lot of times I felt that I just did not have the language to get involved. The language always comes, though, doesn't it—through increased socialization.

Although her undergraduate degree was from USM, Bette credits her experience in her freshman composition class for her decision to major in English and become a teacher.

And when I started, I can remember in my freshman comp class at Alcorn having one teacher who just had a way of listening to our essays, just listening and talking about them, that just inspired me. And after a while, . . . I think it was her example that made me know I wanted to major in English. And then I had some other really strong teachers at Alcorn. Teachers that I felt really comfortable with in ways that I did not feel comfortable at USM. And it was at Alcorn, I think, when I first knew that I was going to be, of course it was, that I was going to be an English teacher. So I really value the education I got at Alcorn.

Motivated by her desire to improve her teaching skills, Bette continued to learn and grow through many different avenues. She has spent many summers working to improve her teaching. Her first summer institute was with the National Writing Project.

Actually, I got involved with it because an assistant principal brought down to my classroom one morning an announcement, a printed announcement with an application. And it was announcing the first summer institute. It described the National Writing Project, and . . . I remember thinking, gosh, this is just what I needed. I had been struggling trying to teach writing, trying to use writing in my classroom all my career. But I really felt the need for some inspiration and some guidance, you know. So he gave me that, said he thought I might be interested, and of course I was. And I applied and I went for an interview. You had to submit a writing sample, you had to do an interview, you had to describe a successful writing lesson that you might be able to present to the whole institute that summer. I did all that and I was accepted. And that was it.

Bette, so successful as a participant in the National Writing Project summer institute, was subsequently invited to serve as a group leader and eventually codirector of the institute. She still values that experience.

> And I think that first summer and the subsequent summers that I spent and the experience I continue to gain through Writing Project has been a really big influence in . . . the satisfaction I have derived from my teaching.

Bette's continuing desire to improve as a teacher led her to participate in several National Endowment for the Humanities (NEH) institutes. Among the topics she studied at the NEH institutes are literary criticism and oral history. True to form, she used these experiences to enhance her teaching. "I learned a lot from that because I used . . . what I learned there to start doing some oral history community research in the high school."

Bette continued to spend her summers learning and growing as an English teacher. Her most recent accomplishments include earning two graduate degrees, an MA (Master of Arts) and an MLitt (Master of Letters) in writing and literacy acquisition from the Bread Loaf School of English. Completing the MA and MLitt degrees afforded Bette the opportunity to study in Vermont; Juneau, Alaska; and Oxford, England. From her Bread Loaf experience, Bette added another facet to her teaching skills.

> Dixie Goswami . . . showed me how and continues to show me how to do classroom-based research, where I really do serious reflection on what goes in my work. Sometimes I get my students to collaborate with me in documenting class events. That way you can . . . more legitimately claim whether or not something is working—you know what I mean?— because you are documenting what's going on all along and its just not about some test score or some other artificial means of evaluation.

Although Bette's work as an educator has been entirely in Mississippi, her educational experiences have brought her in touch with educators from around the country and England in her quest for excellence. Bette is grateful for the opportunities she has had to meet and work with other educators.

> Dixie recommended me about 10, it's been close to 10 years ago, to go to a meeting at Spencer . . . while I was still teaching. . . . Spencer had been

funding traditional research projects, mainly in traditional 4-year colleges, . . . and they wanted to know how they could better fund projects in classrooms of secondary, of grade school teachers, and they also wanted to know a little more about teacher research. So they invited a panel of teachers to meet with them and discuss that. There were about, I'll say about 15 of us from all across the nation. And I was one. . . . So I worked . . . on Spencer projects with a group of teachers, and then of course this last one . . . where I worked with just the project that my students and I did. And I also went to . . . meet with a panel of people from . . . the Dewitt Wallace Foundation. But I learned a lot from just going to invitational conferences like this and meeting teachers from all over the nation who were doing really remarkable things in their classrooms. And I think you learn by association, and I've just been blessed to have had the opportunity to interact with some really great teachers.

Although an award-winning teacher, Bette is not one to rest on her laurels. Her involvement in her many professional opportunities is driven by the desire to be a better teacher.

You know, I'm never quite satisfied with the quality of my work. And I guess that's one reason I work like a fool. But I'm never completely pleased, but maybe there are moments, you know what I'm talking about? There are moments when you say, gosh, that's working. But . . . that doesn't happen nearly as often as it needs to for me. I'm forever trying to do something to make things work better.

A CALLING TO TEACH

Although her early years held dreams of becoming a stenographer and a journalist, Bette believes that she was called to teach.

But if there is such a thing as being called to a career, I think I was called to teaching. Because . . . everything just led me in that direction. I had some very good teacher mentors . . . both in grade school and in college. And then after that, somewhere between then and graduation, I knew that probably the only thing that I could do with a degree in English in Mississippi was to teach. And then by the time I had taught 4 or 5 years, I knew that there was nothing else I'd rather do. So that's the way it happened.

As a child Bette was mentored by the people in her community. Bette credits her mother's influence along with Sunday school teachers and church leaders for fostering in her a desire to achieve. She also had several grade school teachers in Hattiesburg, Mattie Lou Hardy, LaJohn Fielder, Robert Lewis, and Iva Sandifer, who helped lay the foundation for a career in education.

After leaving the public school system of Hattiesburg, Mississippi, Bette continued to enjoy the benefits of many mentors. One of her most influential mentors was her freshman composition instructor at Alcorn.

I think, when you were talking about mentors, I think I mentioned my freshman comp teacher. Her name was Rubenstine Purnell. And she was my comp teacher at Alcorn, the woman . . . who had a way of listening to essays without jumping on your grammar, without jumping into surface matters. She would just listen to you read, then she'd talk about what she heard, and I'm talking about the content. And she would validate you as a writer even as she made recommendations for revision.

Bette also credits her experience with the Writing Project and her mentors there as positively affecting her teaching.

There are a couple of people in particular in Writing Project. One is Dave Roberts, who was a professor at USM, and the other one is Jennie Essel.

   The Writing Project gave me some new ways to look at what students and I do. You had to take responsibility for describing that work and looking closely at student performance because you had to do demo lessons. And the fact that one very strong advocacy in writing projects is that teachers of writing should write themselves. So it got me looking at my own writing and even sharing my writing with students.

Bette's experiences at Bread Loaf expanded her circle of mentors and the positive impact on her teaching. She speaks with gratitude of the people who nurtured her professional development.

Shirley Brice Heath. I studied with Shirley. . . . I took a course with her and then I did an independent study that grew out of her course. And Courtney Cazden. I took one course with her at Oxford. I took the course with her at Bread Loaf [in] Juneau, Alaska. And . . . I did an independent study with her. And these are people who just work, just as busy as they are, I mean

. . . you can e-mail them all night long. You can call on the phone. And . . . when you're with them on a campus, . . . they'll eat lunch with you, eat dinner with you, take you out. They just give so much of themselves to help people. So Courtney Cazden, Dixie Goswami, Shirley Brice Heath, Jacquelyn Jones Royster, and Andrea Lunsford.

Bread Loaf experiences have, of course, found their way into Bette's classes. She particularly remembers a statement made by Jacquelyn Jones Royster.

And I think, when she said that, . . . I think it was on that first day of her course, she said, "I invite you to bring all of yourself into this room," something just happened for me, you know, that made me feel more at ease. I thought what a wonderful thing to say to students. So I started saying that to my writing students, you know, particularly to students in my writing class, but also to students in the literature courses too. But then on some days when kids let it all hang out I wonder if that was a good idea. And then on some days you wonder how much of yourself you are willing [to give], you know. But I understand what she meant. She meant that you should not feel inhibited in your thinking in bringing your real thoughts to the classroom, and I think that is just a good thing, a good invitation to extend to students. Because I think sometimes they do feel that they are confined to what they think you want to hear.

As a result of her Bread Loaf experience with Dixie Goswami, Bette also continues to involve her students in research in her classroom.

Well, the exciting thing about that is that it's not just my inquiry. I have learned, again with Dixie's help, to engage my students in the same kinds of inquiry. Just as I'm looking at what's happening in the classroom, I very often ask one or two of them, in many ways all of them to a certain extent, but for close documentation I have often asked a couple of students in various classes to help me document what's going on. So there are other eyes and ears to help describe what's happening.

Although Bette has had many experiences and many mentors, she sees two pieces of advice as paramount to her career in education.

I mentioned that one of the principles of NWP is that teachers of writing should write themselves. That's one piece of advice that has been very beneficial to me. And the other one came from Dixie G. and that is that teachers and students benefit from systematic reflection and documentation on their classroom practices. In other words, Dixie advises teachers to describe their classroom culture, to describe what happens, particularly in successful lessons, to document the successful lessons with their students and to be ever observant of their own practice and critical of their own practice. That has been probably the best two pieces of advice. I'm sure there are others, but they've made a big difference in my teaching.

BARRIERS

When asked about barriers she may have faced during her career, Bette talks about struggles she has had within her classroom. One struggle involves the curriculum and "parents (and some administrators) who try to censor class texts, often arguing to ban books they haven't read. I fight back!" Bette also faces barriers that students may bring to the classroom. "Other potential barriers that I try to . . . [turn into] learning opportunities are racist attitudes that sometimes cloud thinking and challenge productive dialogues on important issues."

Then there are the barriers that reflect her desire to balance her passion for teaching and learning with a commitment to serve her family, church, and community.

> Yeah, I've had some barriers. . . . And it continues, I think. And I can't stress enough, and I mean it, I feel called to teach. And I feel that I have been blessed in my career. But almost all of my career I've felt, at some point or another, a sort of pull between commitments to my family, to my church, to community service. You know, just pulled between these concerns and my passion for teaching and learning. And you know you wish you could find time or comparable ways to serve all these interests, but you just can't. . . . Sometimes it's hard to maintain a balance among them.

Bette works with adolescent girls in her community because she feels "compelled to serve the community." She is able to give this service and at the same time fulfill her passion for teaching.

> So as far as barriers go, these are, I guess I would call them just tensions. You know there are times when you can sort of connect them one way or

another. For example, I have worked for a long time with adolescent and preadolescent girls in little, I don't want to call them little, character-building things. . . . We would read pieces by African American women. We would go to dinner. We would go to plays. . . . We'd invite people in to talk about social graces or to teach them little arts and crafts; you know, different things. And that way you connect. You're still teaching in a sense; you're serving the community at the same time. But then you've got to go to church and teach Sunday school, and then you've got to do this and that. And after a while all that stuff starts to kinda drive you crazy. That's been my greatest, I don't know if you would call that a barrier.

Regardless of the barriers Bette faced, she met them head on with the determination and spirit that has characterized her career and life. Bette Davis's career reflects the passion, determination, and thirst for knowledge that breeds success. Through it all, Bette remains the prototype of a humble servant, with her focus on her work rather than her many accolades. In reference to her awards and achievements, Bette is always mindful of those who helped her on her journey.

Knowledge is the prime need of the hour.

—Mary McLeod Bethune

9

An Unusual Ascension to the Superintendency

Sharon Richardson by Julia Ballenger

I want to teach students that there are no limits to what they may accomplish if they apply themselves.

—Sharon Richardson

I met Sharon Richardson 7 years ago. She was a beautiful, bronze-skinned African American woman. Sharon was somewhat quiet and didn't hang out with a particular group. She was extremely intelligent, confident in her abilities to lead others, with a beautiful inviting smile that made others feel at ease in her presence. We were both elementary school principals in Northeast Texas. Sharon and I would often visit with each other during our association conferences.

Approximately 4 years ago, I had an opportunity to meet Sharon again. She was a member of the Texas School Improvement Initiative team and had arrived in this small rural school district to assist the state in its accreditation and compliance review. We exchanged hellos and visited with each other, catching up on events that had occurred since our last visit. By now Sharon had moved from elementary principal to secondary principal. She had not aged one bit, and her beautiful smile was still present.

Several years elapsed, and Sharon made it to the top—superintendent of schools. What an achievement! I knew I had to capture her story. Her experiences and contributions must be shared with other aspiring administrators. After all, women of color represent only 1.4% of superintendents in Texas (Texas Education Agency, 1997–98). As Sharon discussed her accomplishments with me, I could hear the pride in her voice. However, she was never boastful and didn't flaunt her accomplishments. When I look at this young woman in her mid-40s, I am amazed that an elementary school has been named in her honor. Wow! Sharon Richardson Elementary School. How does one accomplish all of this in such a short time? Following is an account of her incredible journey.

We began our interview with Sharon describing Union Hill, the district where she has spent most of her life. Union Hill is a rural Class A school district covering 75 square miles in Northeast Texas. Approximately 350 students attend prekindergarten through grade 12. Within the district boundaries are five small communities: Bettie, Bethlehem, Brumley, Perryville, and Simpsonville. The student population is 72% white, 20% African American, 6% Hispanic, and 2% Asian. Union Hill has approximately 70 faculty and staff members, including substitute teachers. The district has been rated Exemplary and Recognized for the last 5 years, the highest two ratings in the state. Union Hill Independent School District offers many of the same opportunities as larger districts. The tax rate is $1.50 with all debts paid off, and the district receives state, local, and federal allocations and applies for additional grants. Teachers are paid an additional $1,000 over state base rate.

Sharon's educational background was that of a young African American female with an unquenchable thirst for knowledge. She was focused on her studies and didn't let anything stand in the way of accomplishing her educational goals.

EDUCATIONAL BACKGROUND

In the late 1960s and early 1970s, many African American female students were looking forward to graduating from high school. The opportunity to leave home, get married, or go to college had finally arrived. Receiving a higher education was a way of escaping the rural Northeast Texas culture, which definitely had racial lines of demarcation, from the schoolhouse to the pulpit. To Sharon, there was never a question of going to college. She looked forward to attending college and obtaining a degree. Unlike many African American females Sharon's age, she yearned to return to her hometown. Because she was an only child, her parents were delighted with her desire to remain close to them.

I am a 1972 graduate of Union Hill High School. My undergraduate studies included elementary music and elementary education. Immediately after graduation, I went to a university close to home and earned a master's degree in music education. After graduate school, I returned to Union Hill and taught elementary music, science, social studies, and English language arts for 3 years. I chose to remain in the Union Hill School District. This is the only district I have worked in. Most people know me, and I know most of the people in the district. I have always tried to treat students as if they were my own. Union Hill has been an excellent workplace for me during the 27 years of my career.

The conversation moves from Sharon's educational background to the impact of mentors on her career.

MENTORING

Sharon's choice to remain at home in familiar surroundings was a significant factor in her career. "I have established credibility in this district. I am an accepted insider. When you are in a small district it is not hard to know everybody." Her mentors believed she had the credentials, knowledge, and skills to get the job done. Sharon accepted the challenge. After all, she was well equipped. She had earned two master's degrees, a midmanagement certificate, and a superintendent certificate. Sharon had demonstrated her abilities as an outstanding student in the district, a devoted parent, an exemplary teacher, and a successful school administrator. All of these characteristics prepared Sharon to become a superintendent. However, not all African American women with these qualities get the opportunity to become a school superintendent. What was different about Sharon's career path to the superintendency?

My first mentors were my classroom teachers. I wanted to become a teacher so that I could work with children. Nothing in my childhood caused me to want to be an administrator. It was my mentors who encouraged me to believe in myself. They were always there to support me.

My principal saw leadership abilities in me. I guess I demonstrated great classroom management skills. After my first 3 years of teaching, my principal encouraged me to go back to school and get my midmanagement certification. My principal was my mentor. Even though I had a master's degree in music education, I went back to school and earned another master's in secondary education and educational leadership. After serving as elementary and junior high and senior high school principal for 17 years, my superintendent encouraged me to go back to school and work on my superintendent certification. I attended Texas A&M University at Commerce, Texas, and earned my superintendent certification. It was my superintendent who recommended me to the board of trustees for the superintendent's job. My appointment as superintendent was a history-making event. I became the first female superintendent in this school district, and I was also the first African American superintendent in this district.

"Much has been written about the glass-ceiling—that invisible, seemingly impenetrable barrier that blocks women from progressing to higher levels of management. The lack of proportional representation of women combines with even a greater lack of representation by women of color" (Hernandez, 1998). Sharon was able to penetrate the glass ceiling with the help of wonderful mentors, with strong family support, and by being prepared when the opportunity presented itself.

FAMILY TIES THAT BIND

To some aspiring administrators, family can be seen as a barrier or a support mechanism. For Sharon, family served as an important support structure.

I am a divorcee with one child. My son will tell you that school comes first. My son, Byron, is a junior at the University of Texas in Austin, majoring in corporate communication/business. I am proud of all of my son's accomplishments in life. He has succeeded against all odds. My mother, my most important mentor, assisted me in raising Byron. My job required long work hours. I was away from home most of his childhood, but my mother filled in and was there for Byron. I could not have reached the goals I set for myself without my mother. She was always there for me. Both of my parents are now deceased. However, all of my family members and friends have been very supportive of my career choice. That makes a big difference.

Sharon's voice sounded sad. When asked if she would have changed anything in her life, she replied, "No, I have accomplished the goals that I set for myself. I have not experienced any significant barriers while working in this district. I have had excellent support from the school board, fellow administrators, faculty, staff, and parental groups."

The conversation now turns to Sharon's leadership styles.

LEADERSHIP STYLES

The leadership style of most African American women can be described as nurturing but directive, participatory, and inclusive. Sharon's style is no different. She meets with the board, faculty, staff, and students and articulates her vision for the district at the beginning of each new year. She also explains the goals and objectives of the district to each group.

> I have high expectations for my faculty, staff, and students. I require that all faculty and staff set high expectations for all student groups. I am very straightforward. Goals and objectives are developed according to the district's needs. At the beginning of each school year, I meet with all district employees. First, I meet with the school board and review my expectations and goals so that we will share the same vision for the district. During staff development days, I hold general meetings with faculty and staff. I also meet with various student groups from each campus. All groups share a common vision, to improve student performance in all academic areas. We work together collaboratively, challenging students to think critically and perceive the world in various ways. Upon graduation, we would like students to be successful in their lifelong endeavors and goals.

When asked to describe the leadership style that has been most effective for her, Sharon responds:

> I find myself most effective when I am direct, sharing my vision and goals up front. In the process of evaluating my job performance, board members and fellow administrators have stated, "She is intelligent and uses a collaborative

approach to decisions whenever possible. She sets high standards for herself, and others. She always expects the most from everyone and genuinely cares for the people of this district."

Sharon's story ends with a description of her daily schedule. In a rural school district, the superintendent wears many hats. Sharon begins the day at 7:30 A.M. and ends around 4:30 P.M.

When there are extracurricular activities such as ball games or board meetings, I stay at school until 9:00 or 10:00 P.M. I attend numerous meetings during the school year. I am responsible for many tasks, which include, but are not limited to, working closely with the board of trustees, working with staff on curriculum planning, managing personnel and administrators, attending to facility needs, and working closely with parents and community groups. I feel my most important duties are the daily recommendations I make concerning policies, involving district finance, institutional programs, student issues, and school facilities issues. I prepare the annual budget and ensure that sound, consistent practices are utilized in the operation of the district. The administrators work closely together as a team. Our motto is: "Striving for excellence in academic achievement." I think of myself as being blessed and honored to be the superintendent of Union Hill Independent School District. I want to be a role model for all students. I want to teach students that there are no limits to what they may accomplish if they apply themselves. Education is a necessity. I feel like I am needed in this rural area in order to see that all students have an opportunity to be successful. I always tell students to reach for the stars, the sky is the limit.

FUTURE GOALS

As Sharon and I ended our conversation, I asked about her future goals. She smiled and said, "I have a contract with the district for the next 5 years. At the end of the contract, I can retire with full benefits." Will this outstanding African American woman retire in 5 years? I would guess "no." I can envision Sharon moving from public education to higher education. What better person than this outstanding educational leader to spend the remainder of her life helping to prepare future administrators.

Sharon closed our interview by citing a quote that best describes her: "Some people dream of success, while others wake up and work hard at it. I've always had to work hard at achieving success." Sharon's hard work certainly paid off.

> You need only claim the events of your life to make yourself your own. When you truly possess all you have been and done . . . you are fierce with reality.
>
> —Florida Scott-Maxwell, *The Measure of My Days*

10

Born to Teach

Dawn Shelton-Mitchell by Faye Hicks-Townes

I really and truly believe that God has given me a purpose here, and I
try to do the best I can.

—Dawn Shelton-Mitchell

Dawn Shelton-Mitchell has taught in the Detroit public school system
for 25 years and sees her career as "truly a blessing." The recipient of numerous awards for teaching and community service, Dawn's "goal has
always been to reach the child that others have given up on." She has
chosen to work with autistic children because many people do give up on
them, and they present a unique challenge.

> And the children, I've found that many of them have great talent in those
> areas, but it does require quite a bit. And I think that's one reason I went into
> autism because I get a chance to use all areas of my endorsements in the
> classroom (LD, EMI, TMI, SMI, EI, orthopedic impairment, and autism) to
> reach my students.

While the challenge of bringing out the best in a student with so many
obstacles would be daunting to most, Dawn seems to thrive on it. Her
"philosophy of teaching is that given the right tool every child can
achieve, every child can learn." An example Dawn gives is of a student
"who was nonverbal, didn't talk, couldn't talk." Dawn continued to work
with and encourage him until he left for high school, "and it was just
amazing, he went out doing very, very well."

Dawn's success in the classroom is also evidenced by her students' desire to be present every day. With an attendance record of almost 100 percent, Dawn shares that "the parents say that even when the children have a cold they insist that they have to come to school." Although Dawn is appreciative of the awards and accolades she receives from the parents of her students, she sees being able to work with her students as a reward in itself.

> It's rewarding, and the parents say how much I'm a blessing to them and their children. And I share with them, you don't know how much a blessing your child is to me.

CALLED AT AN EARLY AGE

Like many other educators, Dawn decided at a very early age that she wanted to teach. She was only 7 years old when she knew she wanted to become a teacher. This interest in teaching stemmed from her desire to serve others.

> Well, as a very young child I decided that teaching was for me. Either working with younger children or working with the elderly. It's always been an interest, helping someone who really needed the help, most of my life.

It is not a surprise that Dawn was interested in helping others. She grew up in a household that stressed caring and giving. "You know, it stems from my parents both being caring, giving people. And that was what our household was based on, helping others and helping those who cannot help themselves." Dawn's parents' example of service was contagious.

> My eldest sister taught school, and my brother helped others learning to use the computers. I have an identical twin sister, and she's in special ed too. She's been teaching 25 years as well, but she stayed in emotionally impaired. We had one sister that's under us, so we're a year apart. And the three of us, that's what we did most of the time. You know, finding some child to tutor. Another example is my youngest sister. She and her husband adopted nine children.

A childhood spent in a home environment that stressed service and caring has become a legacy that Dawn has passed on to her daughters.

BALANCING FAMILY AND WORK

Many professionals have the problem of trying to balance career and family. Dawn is no exception in that respect. To avoid the conflict of choosing whether to spend time with her daughters or with her students, Dawn brought the two together. "I think that was one way of tying it all together, . . . to bring my children in so that they saw how important the job was."

Dawn not only gave her children an awareness of the importance of teaching by bringing them into her classroom, she also gave them an opportunity to serve.

> They had the music classes and dance classes and all that. What they learned they would come in and share that experience and help the children. I had one child who enjoyed dancing, so my daughter taught her a dance that she could perform on the stage. So although they were special needs, the children always participate in whatever the school has. They know that we're on program just like the others. So I just use whatever talent they have to help.

Although Dawn encouraged her daughters to volunteer at the school, that serving spirit was soon evident in their actions.

> Because they always had to come over to the school to volunteer their service for half days or when they had a break. In fact the first two times I asked them, but the other times they volunteered to come on over and help out the children.

That early experience has had a lasting impact on her daughters. Although Dawn wanted her oldest daughter to become an engineer, her daughter told Dawn that her "hope and dream has always been to teach too." She is now a math teacher and still comes over to help Dawn with her students. She always keeps an eye open for ideas that can enhance student learning.

Dawn's youngest daughter, in her first year of college at age 17, exemplifies her mother's model of service.

> In fact even now, my youngest in school makes sure she sends information to help out the children, and my oldest comes over. When I was doing academic games, each week she would come over and do something to help the children.

Her youngest daughter's future plan also reflects a home environment that stressed "caring about others."

> My youngest has already talked about opening up a dance school. That's what her major is, dance therapy and sports medicine. But she . . . [has shared] with the family how hard it is to get someone to take the autistic children in the community, to work with them . . . in music or what have you because everyone can't teach them.

Dawn, also by example, taught her daughters the importance of education. As she worked on her master's degrees and endorsement, she modeled being a good student for her children by making sure that "while they were doing their homework I was doing mine."

By involving her children in her work, Dawn achieved balance in her work and family life responsibilities. She also provided opportunities for her students to learn and grow while at the same time gave her daughters opportunities to learn and share. By combining her two worlds, family and work, she enriched both.

ALWAYS MORE TO LEARN

Dawn began her undergraduate career at Wayne State University. She completed a 5-year degree majoring in the education of mentally impaired, homebound, and orthopedically impaired students. Since that time, Dawn has gone on to earn two master's degrees. Both master's degrees, one in learning disabilities and the other in working with the emotionally impaired, were earned at Wayne State University.

Continually working to improve herself as an educator, Dawn has earned an educational specialist degree from Wayne State University and currently holds all but three certification endorsements in special education. She is influenced by the needs of her students and her own desire to learn. Even though Dawn did not have to, she decided to go back and get an endorsement in autism.

> Well, each time I had a child that was on a different level or it appeared that I needed to reach a different child, and from 1988 on it was due to enhancing my own learning habits, having to learn all over again. But when I was going for the two master's, it was trying to learn more to help the children.

Dawn's desire to give her students the best leads her to learn in many different settings. She attends workshops for professional development. "You know, I'm always at workshops because I don't think you can ever get enough. I really don't." She even uses her hobbies as a resource for her students.

> Sewing I did for a long while. And I made my clothes a good while. But again, I was just taking up, it's always been [about] taking up something that would enhance the other students' learning. So I did small hobbies just to learn, so I could teach the children.

It is evident that Dawn is motivated to help her students, and this guides her in every aspect of her life. Although Dawn has several degrees and endorsements, her future plans still include more education. She intends to begin a PhD program in educational administration to pursue yet another goal. "My goal is once I retire to open up my own special needs school. . . . That's what I did one of my master's theses on, and I've been just adding to it, bits and pieces of information."

Dawn truly epitomizes the character of a lifelong learner. That learning is used to enrich the lives of the students she serves. She says, "And I think maybe, I'm sure there are other careers too, but I know it's one where there is never too much learning."

STAYING FOCUSED

Once Dawn is in the classroom, her focus is on the students. Just as she focuses on the needs of her students in choosing educational pursuits and hobbies, Dawn lets nothing come between her and her students' learning in the classroom. Her colleagues at the school know that about her and respect it.

> Everybody knows you don't come to room 322 with any conversation. You meet me after school. Not even on the lunch break because there are things I've got to prepare for the afternoon, and everyone respects that.

This strong and focused work ethic has influenced those who work with Dawn. As she continues to model putting the students first, her peers notice and "it has changed a lot of them. They do the same thing."

The guiding philosophy of Dawn's dedication to her work and her students is explained when she puts herself in the parents' shoes.

> I tell them one thing that I think, what has gotten me all the way through is that I think, "If it were my child, would I want it done?" And that's how I do it. I don't want, you know, when you're supposed to be teaching my child, I don't want you holding conversations and not being with them. And so they understand when I put it to them and say, "Now if I were teaching your child, would you want me to be having conversations?" Case closed.

Dawn believes "that children are very important," so she extends that same care and concern she has for her students to all the students in the school. She does that through interacting with students and providing a positive climate in and around her classroom.

> You know what? I've noticed in life that if you try to help others it definitely comes back. I don't only work with my special needs children, I try to be a counselor, a social worker for every child who comes past, who comes my way. . . . And I try to put a message, some type of positive message around my door, on the outside of the door of the classroom. And of course it's all in the classroom. But something about autism so that the children can learn the difference, the children's special needs, what have you. So when they're mainstreamed in the classes they don't have a problem. And the regular ed children definitely look out for the students, for my students.

As part of a learning community and lead teacher for special education and regular teachers, Dawn is always eager and willing to share her experience and expertise with others. She devotes time and energy to training and workshops for the special education faculty. Dawn's "supervisors know that whatever [the] area of special ed, . . . they can send someone over to be helped." Not only her peers but also student teachers have learned from Dawn. Although the student teachers are learning from her, Dawn views their presence in her classroom as an asset.

> I don't want to constantly say [it], but it's just a blessing to have someone help the children. I guess when you've been in this situation as long as I have and see things that really need to be fixed, it's nice when they come in. People are wanting to be helped and people can help the children. That's quite rewarding to me.

Dawn's devotion to her teaching is evidenced in the professionalism and caring she models for her students, future teachers, and colleagues.

WORDS OF WISDOM

Although Dawn has been and is an example to many, there have been people in her life who influenced her. Her parents provided a nurturing household that fostered a philosophy of caring and service to others. In the area of education, Dawn mentions two people, an older sister and her high school English teacher.

> Besides my parents and an older sister who passed away who was also in education—I'm very, very proud of her, and she did quite a bit of mentoring to me as well as to others—there was a teacher in high school . . . Ms. Waters, an English teacher I'll never forget. She really set high standards. In fact she's one that I'll never forget.

When asked about the advice that has influenced her, Dawn talks about an uncle:

> That I finally started listening to? Don't put yourself last; you know, always count yourself. I never shall forget I had an uncle that would always say that I do for others more than I do for myself. And my uncle, who has passed away now, always said don't you ever say that again. I want you to always think of yourself first so that you can help others. And my parents always said the same thing, but you know they were always doing for others. And

I don't know, it just became a habit. But I recall my uncle's last few days of life. He wanted to make sure that he stressed that to me. I love myself and take care of myself because if I don't do it for myself then I definitely won't be able to do it for others.

This advice seems contradictory in light of Dawn's life. Even now when considering an opportunity to teach courses at the university, something she would do for herself, Dawn is hesitant, putting thoughts of her students first.

You know I'm really considering doing it, but right now, as I shared, my main focus is getting this last group through high school, getting them to high school. But I have discussed it with the family, and we're talking about doing something for myself for once. . . . And that's why I'm thinking strongly about doing it. All of my life I have been giving to others, and as I said it's been quite rewarding so . . . I don't resent it, but I'm trying to put myself on my schedule for once.

STRENGTH FROM ADVERSITY

Barriers come in many forms, and how we respond to them makes a world of difference. When I asked Dawn about barriers in her career, she did not hesitate. Her barrier was a life-threatening attack by a parent.

In 1988, February 5th of 1988, I was assaulted by an irate parent who . . . stated that she had waited 3 years to get me as her child's teacher, and once again I put another child in her child's spot. She had come up to the school to kill me. But when she pulled the gun out, the daughter hollered, "Momma, please don't kill her!" I was severely beaten, and all I can remember now is the children fighting her off and the child's teacher committing suicide. It almost took the dream I had. In fact the doctors had mentioned that due to my assault and being beaten in the head I could not obtain or hold any information. They shared with my family that they had to get used to me being the way I was. Which meant that I was permanently disabled.

Although Dawn was seriously injured by this attack, she did not let it end her career.

I was out of work for a while. But I was determined that I could not let any-one take the joy that I had. And the mother came back and stated that she was sorry, that she just meant to scare me. . . . It took a long while to get over that. And what it makes me think, even if you do well, it doesn't mean that you won't have barriers in your life. And that was one that almost took my joy and my thunder. But through the grace of God I came back and came back strong. I did get many endorsements and an ed specialist [certificate], so it proved the doctors wrong, many doctors wrong, as well as the other evil forces that were out there.

Dawn's successful comeback from her attack is a testament to her de-termination and faith. She not only recovered physically, but she also went on to earn another degree and other endorsements in special education. She has used this experience to motivate her to achieve even more.

It's one that reminds me that things could be worse than they are. And it def-initely helped me turn negatives into positives, which is what I've done most of my life but even more so now. . . . That is why I really and truly be-lieve that God has given me a purpose here, and I try to do the best I can.

Dawn continues to work with autistic children in the Detroit public school system. Modeling a philosophy that respects every child and be-lieves every child can learn, Dawn continues a legacy of caring. Always ready to help and share her wealth of knowledge and experience, she re-mains a rich source for preservice and practicing teachers. For Dawn, her career continues to be "a blessing."

Service is the rent we pay for living. It is the very purpose of life and not something you do in your spare time.

—Marian Wright Edelman

***

Memories of our lives, of our works and our deeds will continue in others.

—Rosa Parks

11

Building a Bridge to Ourselves

Sandra Harris

The stories that fill these pages are about "winning" women who have won recognition for their contributions to education—women who are leaders as superintendents, principals, and teachers. But these stories are really much more complex. Parker Palmer (1993) points out, "The interview, that favorite tool of social data gatherers, is meant to be an 'interview,' a way of looking into other people's behaviors and attitudes that opens our own lives to view" (p. 62). And these stories do just that, whether we have been recognized as award winners or not. As these nine women open up their lives to share their experiences, their stories create a bridge to our own stories.

We began this project by identifying nine women who have formally been acknowledged as leaders, and we asked them to share their lives with us. We asked many questions including queries about their childhood, work ethic and career path, mentoring opportunities, leadership styles, and personal and professional barriers. As we read and study their stories, it becomes apparent that each story is different, yet each story is the same. Dawn Smith's story is one of dedication to building a safe sense of community for children. Sandra's story resonates with achievement and the importance of being encouraged to achieve. Molly shares her passionate focus on high standards for herself, for her faculty, and for children. Donnya's story is rich with determination as she opens new vistas for leaders to follow. Joy energetically flows from Patsy's story—the joy of living, giving, and doing. Candace tells a story that is rich with creativity focused on improving schools for children. Bette is called to teach and continues to focus on excellence in learning for herself and others. Sharon's story stresses the importance of setting goals for oneself and the influence this can have on a school district. Dawn Shelton-Mitchell's story resonates with her life of service for others.

From our questions, many side themes emerged, such as an early love of learning, a strong work ethic, and the importance of mentoring. However, three major leadership themes connected all of these stories: (1) joy—these women lead with joy and find a deep, abiding joy in serving others; (2) excellence—these women are clearly focused on standards of excellence for all; and (3) spirituality—these women have a sense of power nurtured in spirituality.

JOY: FINDING A DEEP, ABIDING JOY IN SERVING OTHERS

All of our women leaders revealed that from the earliest times, they had strong, nurturing home support from family members, generally mothers and grandmothers, who instilled a love of learning and a desire to achieve, as well as an understanding of hard work. Several pointed out that one of their earliest memories centered around books and reading, and as children they found great joy in reading. Bette remembers walking "the mile to our little 'branch' of the town's public library" when she was only 9 years old, and she recalls some of the poetry she would read.

Even as youngsters, it was clear that these women, for the most part, felt called to the service of teaching. Dawn Smith said that from "the beginning she knew that she wanted to be a teacher." While Sandra often played at being teacher, complete with her own grade book, Candace told about teaching children, even as a child of 10. Bette said that she "was called to teach," while Dawn Shelton-Mitchell expressed that she was "born to teach."

The Importance of Being Helped and Helping Others

All the women noted the importance of mentoring. Each was mentored by family members growing up. Professionally, however, they were mentored by other teachers and, more important, by men and women who already held key leadership positions. Invariably these principals, superintendents, and university deans noticed the leadership qualities of these women and encouraged them to pursue greater challenges. Further, by placing the women in positions of greater power, the mentors contributed to their success. For example, Sandra Lowery described how her superintendent pointed out the importance of achieving the superintendency through the high school principalship. When this position was available, with his support, she became a high school principal. Patsy Hallman noted that the previous dean paved the way for her to move into this position.

But mentoring actually played an even more important role in the women's lives. In addition to opening up opportunities for them, it also made them sensitive to their own need to give back and mentor others. Thus, while they talked about the importance of mentoring to achieve greater positions of leadership, they also shared their own commitment to mentoring others. For example, Molly spends a "good portion of her day coaching and mentoring principals and other school leaders." Mentoring others has been an important leadership role for Donnya and Patsy, as well.

Joy comes from doing a job that people love, and it is obvious through all these stories that joy abounds in the jobs they do. Candace describes it as the best and most rewarding work in the world because of the opportunity to guide generations of children. When parents tell Dawn Shelton-Mitchell that she is "a blessing to them and their children," she insists that they can't know "how much a blessing your child is to me." Frederick Buechner (1993) defines vocation as "the place where your deep gladness and the world's deep hunger meet" (p. 119)—such is the joy of a well-loved job done well.

EXCELLENCE: STANDARDS OF EXCELLENCE FOR ALL

Talk of standards of excellence in education today occurs so often that we were reluctant to use the word *excellence* for fear it would seem common. However, a standard of excellence is clearly obvious in all the stories.

Excellence Standard for Themselves

While all of the women talk about the importance of having a high standard for children, it is evident through the stories of their childhoods that even as very young children, they were held to a standard of excellence. For example, Molly recounts taking music lessons and competing in athletic events as a youngster. Donnya tells of having a grandmother who required the children to "hold a book for an hour by a kerosene lamp" even if their lessons had been completed at school.

Bette is driven toward excellence by her desire to be a better teacher. She says that she is "never quite satisfied with the quality" of her work and admits, "I'm forever trying to do something to make things work better." Dawn Shelton-Mitchell is going back to work on a doctorate because of her own desire to learn and eventually open a school for children with special needs.

Being More Excellent than Others Is Often a Necessity for Women

Some of the focus on excellence is from necessity. Donnya tells of racial barriers she encountered at the university: "I was looked upon as an African American female professor to the faculty and to my students. Every day I walked into the classroom I had to prove to my students that I was worthy of having this position." Molly emphasizes that for women to be considered for leadership roles they must "be clearly outstanding. . . . Women must be well prepared to compete." Sandra remembers a conversation with a gentleman in her community who could not understand why a wife and mother would be driving several hours a day to the university to earn a doctorate.

Work Ethic

A standard of excellence is obvious in the work ethic exhibited by every one of the nine women. They all speak of long days and exhausting struggles to accomplish all that should be accomplished. Most of them do this while also having families and raising their own children. There is no doubt that the workday of a leader is long. In Sandra's words, it is from "can 'til can't." Molly describes herself as a "workaholic." Candace began her day as a principal by 4:30 A.M. in order to exercise because she knew that once the day began at school, exercise would not be possible. She frequently did not return home until after 10:00 P.M. This long workday and the nature of a leader's job, which is never done, prompt Patsy to encourage and advise other women to use their time wisely and be resourceful.

Passion for Excellence for Children

As the women begin discussing their drive for excellence to improve schools for children, their stories resonate with passion. Dawn Smith speaks of the problems of education on the reservation, yet student achievement has steadily improved under her leadership. Molly describes the school improvement process as one of riding the rapids and repeatedly shares her belief of how important it is to "work to achieve a high-quality education for every child."

Candace describes the excitement of creating "her dream"—an arts magnet school—and recounts that she "wrote continually for 6 weeks, . . . even waking in the middle of the night." Bette's desire for excellence begins with herself, but it extends to her teaching to provide the best for students. Through her commitment to excellence, Sharon has "established credibility" and has become an "accepted insider," all because she had the credentials, knowledge, and skills to do an excellent job. Dawn Shelton-Mitchell has chosen to extend a standard of excellence to children with autism because so many people give up on them. Her motivation to help students guides every aspect of her life.

The search for excellence is a powerful search. According to Max De-Pree (1989), "Our search for elegance, for completeness, for our potential is a search that should not end. What a marvelous horizon!" (p. 134). This search for excellence keeps us growing. Several years ago, a cigarette advertisement targeting women said, "You've come a long way, baby!" We have, but the quest for excellence keeps us moving on and on and on.

SPIRITUALITY: A SENSE OF POWER NURTURED IN SPIRITUALITY

As the women in our study shared their stories, they mentioned barriers, sacrifices, sense of community, empowerment, and opportunities, often within the same thought. They obviously saw all of these issues as connected rather than in isolation. Through their discussions, it was clear that

their sense of self and sense of power in handling both barriers and opportunities of leadership were rooted in a strong spirituality.

Cultural Barriers

Within their communities, our winning women often faced cultural barriers caused by gender as well as color; often the distinction is unclear. For
example, Dawn Smith speaks about "being brown"; she does not know
whether barriers were due to gender or skin color, but the school board refused her first application to become principal at the elementary school.
Molly was simply told by her superintendent that the district was "not
ready for a woman." Donnya sat on committees at the university, but her
voice was not heard. Sandra was called "the Skirt" when she was principal at the high school. Most of our women were place-bound. They commuted to universities; they commuted to jobs. Patsy failed to look for a
deanship, although she qualified, because she could not leave the area.
Molly voices the loneliness of the leadership role because the support network is so small.

Personal Barriers

Families sacrificed, yet, by and large, supported them in their quest to become leaders. The time needed to do the important job of leadership and
to do it well took a toll on families in many ways—loss of time together,
strain on relationships, eating lots of peanut butter sandwiches—but almost invariably these women describe how these sacrifices brought a
stronger family commitment to their vision. For example, Dawn Shelton-
Mitchell describes how even her two daughters committed to careers
working with children, an outgrowth of their mother's influence.

Sense of Community

Developing a sense of community was a guiding, passionate vision that
grew out of an almost spiritual desire to bring people together. In every
case, the goal was to make education better for children. Whether it was
forging a respect for the school within the community as in Dawn Smith's
case, creating a writing community where children could express their

feelings safely as in Bette's classroom, or in leading a district to excel as in Molly's case, repeatedly, the importance of a sense of community was articulated in their stories.

This sense of community was created through an understanding of empowerment that was collaborative and collegial. While the leadership styles differed in each unique circumstance, each woman cultivated a team of professionals on her campus and invited parents to be part of the school leadership team. While Donnya says, "I lead from behind," others were clearly more directed. For example, Sharon points out that she is "most effective when I am direct, sharing my vision and goals up front." Sandra notes that she started out as a very directive leader but soon learned to rely on the wisdom and expertise of her faculty as she became more collaborative in her approach to leadership.

Whether discussing barriers, opportunities, or leadership styles, the women in this study chose to identify life issues as "simply realities that . . . would take action to overcome, not realities that sealed" their fates, as Patsy notes. Through everything, their sense of self and faith seemed to come from a well of spirituality that provided courage, energy, and wisdom. Thus opportunities were created and barriers overcome. Molly emphasizes that her courage "is in response to God's abiding love." Patsy talks of a strong faith and her commitment to her church. Dawn Shelton-Mitchell recounts "the grace of God" in helping her overcome barriers. While Dawn Smith describes herself as not being very spiritual, on the advice of a friend, she started every day by going outside at dawn and looking up at the stars. She would talk to the stars about "helping me through the day, and doing the best thing." When she told this to her friend, the friend was appalled. She had wanted her to take time to reflect and "to look up and give thanks for the day you have to make a difference in lives." In other words, her friend wanted Dawn to say thank you for the opportunity to make a difference in people's lives.

A sense of spirituality runs like a silent stream throughout these stories. Palmer (1998) notes that "the connections made by good teachers are held not in their methods but in their hearts—meaning 'heart' in its ancient sense, as the place where intellect and emotion and spirit and will converge in the human self." They acknowledge their strength from a spiritual source; they overcome barriers by drawing on this source; and they create their approach to leadership based on their sense of commitment to something larger than themselves.

CONCLUSION

The process of sharing stories has been a living example of Jacquelyn Jones Royster's invitation to "bring all of yourself into this room." These nine award-winning women educators have permitted us a glimpse into their lives. In so doing, they bring to life a new understanding of leadership that enriches our own quest. All nine of our women leaders are teachers. They began as teachers and they continue today as teachers. Through their stories, we see that leadership and the art of good teaching are eternally connected by a deep, abiding joy in serving others, by a focus on standards of excellence for all, and by power nurtured in spirituality. Through their stories we build a bridge to ourselves.

References

Ah Nee-Benham, M., & Cooper, J. (1998). *Let my spirit soar! Narrative of diverse women in school leadership.* Thousand Oaks, CA: Corwin.

Allison, M. (2000, September 11). Bank on women: Few females rise to top but conditions improving. *San Antonio Express–News*, p. F1.

Banks, J., & Banks, C. (1995). *Handbook of research on multicultural education.* New York: Macmillan.

Barnett, R. (1971). Personality correlates of vocational planning. *Genetic Psychology Monographs, 83,* 309–356.

Bartlett, J. (1938). *Familiar quotations* (11th ed.). Boston: Little, Brown & Co.

Bass, B. (1990). *Bass & Stogdill's handbook of leadership: A survey of theory and research* (3rd ed.). New York: Free Press.

Bloom, L., & Munro, P. (1995). Conflicts of selves: Nonunitary subjectivity in women administrators' life history narratives. In J. A. Hatch & R. Wisniewski (Eds.), *Life history and narrative* (pp. 99–112). London: Falmer.

Blount, J. (1998). *Destined to rule the schools: Women and the superintendency, 1873–1995.* Albany: State University of New York Press.

Buechner, F. (1993). *Wishful thinking: A seeker's ABC.* San Francisco: Harper.

Collins, P. H. (1990). *The politics of black feminist thought.* In P. Collins & P. Hill (Eds.), *Black feminist thought: Knowledge, consciousness, and the politics of empowerment* (pp. 3–18). New York: Routledge.

Colwill, N. (1997). Women in management: Power and powerlessness. In D. Dunn (Ed.), *Workplace/women's place: An anthology* (pp. 186–197). Los Angeles: Roxbury.

Coontz, S. (2000). Marriage: Then and now. *Phi Kappa Phi Journal, 8*(3), 10–15.

Cooper, J., & Heck, R. (1995). Using narrative in the study of school administration. *International Journal of Qualitative Research in Education, 8*(2), 195–210.

Costello, C., & Stone, A. J. (Eds.) (1994). *The American woman: 1994–1995.* New York: W.W. Norton.

DePree, M. (1989). *Leadership is an art.* New York: Doubleday.

DeRamus, B. (1999, February). Living legends: African American woman heroes. *Essence Magazine* [Online]. Available: http://www.findarticles.com.

Ezrati, J. (1983). Personnel policies in higher education: A covert means of sex discrimination? *Educational Administration Quarterly, 19*(4), 105–119.

Gilligan, C. (1977). In a different voice: Women's conceptions of self and morality. *Harvard Educational Review, 47,* 481–517.

Gilligan, C. (1993). *In a different voice: Psychological theory and women's development.* Cambridge, MA: Harvard University Press.

Glass, T. (1992). *The study of the American school superintendency 1992: America's educational leaders in a time of reform.* Arlington, VA: American Association of School Administrators.

Glass, T., Bjork, L., & Brunner, C. (2000). *The study of the American superintendency: 2000.* Arlington, VA: American Association of School Administrators.

Grogan, M. (2000). Laying the groundwork for a reconception of the superintendency from feminist postmodern perspectives. *Educational Administration Quarterly, 36*(1), 117–142.

Harris, S., Arnold, M., Lowery, S., & Marshall, R. (2001). A study of educators in commuter marriages. *Planning and Changing, 32*(1 & 2), 114–123.

Hensel, N. (1991). *Realizing gender equality in higher education: The need to integrate work/family issues.* Washington, DC: ERIC Clearinghouse on Higher Education. (ERIC Document Reproduction Service No. ED 340 273)

Hernandez, Y. (1998, May). Intercultural Development Research Association newsletter. San Antonio, TX: Intercultural Development Research Association.

Holtkamp, L. (2002). Crossing borders: An analysis of the characteristics and attributes of female public school principals. *Advancing Women in Leadership Journal 10*(1) [Online]. Available: http://www.advancingwomen.com/awl/winter2002/holtkamp.html.

Hudson, J., & Rea, D. (1998). Teachers' perceptions of women in the principalship: A current perspective. *Advancing Women in Leadership Journal, 1*(3) [Online]. Available: http://www.advancingwomen.com/awl/summer98/HUD.html.

Irby, B., Brown, G., & Trautman, D. (1999). Equalizing opportunities: Analysis of current leadership theory and its relationship to a feminine inclusive leadership theory. In F. English & P. Jenlink (Eds.), *School leadership: Expanding horizons of the mind and spirit* (pp. 168–178). Lancaster, PA: Technomic.

Jamieson, K. (1995). *Beyond the double bind: Women and leadership.* Oxford: Oxford University Press.

Johnson, J. J. (1973). Why administrators fail. *Clearing House, 48,* 3–6.

Jones, D. (2003, January 27). Few women hold top executive jobs, even when CEOs are female. *USA Today,* pp. B1, B2.

Lowery, S., & Harris, S. (2001). Being a woman AND a superintendent. In B. Irby & G. Brown (Eds.), *Conference proceedings: Research on Women and Education 26th Annual Conference* (pp. 158–177). Huntsville, TX: Sam Houston State University.

Morgan, R. (1993). *The word of a woman: Feminist dispatches 1968–1992.* New York: Norton.

Natale, J. (1992). Up the career ladder. *The Executive Educator, 14*(2), 16–23.

Orenstein, P. (2000). *Flux: Women on sex, work, kids, love, and life in a half-changed world.* New York: Doubleday.

Ortiz, F. I. (1982). *Career patterns in educational administration: Women, men and minorities in educational administration.* New York: Praeger.

Ortiz, F. I., & Marshall, C. (1988). Women in educational administration. In N. Boyan (Ed.), *Handbook of research on educational administration* (pp. 123–142). New York: Longman.

Palmer, P. (1993). *To know as we are known: Education as a spiritual journey.* San Francisco: Harper.

Palmer, P. (1998). *The courage to teach: Exploring the inner landscape of a teacher's life.* San Francisco: Jossey-Bass.

Pankake, A. (1995). Mirrors, brick walls, and see-through panels: An exploration of some of the barriers to leadership opportunities for women. In B. Irby & G. Brown (Eds.), *Women as school executives: Voices and visions* (pp. 185–189). Huntsville, TX: Texas Council of Women School Executives.

Ramsey, R. D. (1997). On the personal side: Domestic relationships of the superintendency. *School Administrator, 54*(6), 36–39.

Saks, J. (1992, December). Education vital signs. *American School Board Journal, 179*(12), 32–45.

Shakeshaft, C. (1989). *Women in educational administration.* Newbury Park, CA: Corwin Press.

Smith, L. (2000, September 2). Trailing wife often limits her career, study suggests. *San Antonio Express–News,* 1H–2H.

Steffy, B. (2002). Women in the superintendency: Leadership for changing times. In H. Sobehart (Ed.), *2002 monograph of the Women Administrators Conference: Leadership in changing times.* Duquesne, IL: School of Education Leadership Institute and the American Association of School Administrators.

Sullivan, J. (2003, June 22). Guiding principal. *Sunday Oregonian,* pp. A14–A15.

Texas Education Agency (1997–98). Texas public school districts including charter schools, table 1—fall, 1990–98: FTE counts by personnel types and subtypes by sex and ethnicity—state total. Austin, TX: Author.

Tozer, S., Violas, P. C., & Senese, G. B. (1998). *School and society: Historical and contemporary perspectives* (3rd ed.). Boston: McGraw-Hill.

U.S. Census Bureau. (1998). *Statistical abstract of the United States: 199.* (119th ed.) Washington, DC: Author.

Walth, B., Christensen, K., & Sullivan, J. (2003, December 7). A place where children die. *Oregonian.* [Online].

Zemlicka, B. (2001). *The career paths of Texas public school superintendents.* Unpublished dissertation, College Station, Texas A&M University.

About the Authors

Sandra Harris is an associate professor in the Educational Leadership Department at Lamar University in Beaumont, Texas. She received her Ph.D. from The University of Texas at Austin after 25 years as a public and private school teacher and administrator. Her research has focused on standards-based school leader preparation, gender studies, social justice issues, and K–12 peer harassment. Dr. Harris is editor of the National Council of Professors of Educational Administration *Education Leadership Review.* In addition to publishing many journal articles, she has also coauthored three case study books for superintendents, principals, and assistant principals and a book on bullying. She has edited a book on schools of choice. Her most recent book is *BRAVO Principal! Building Relationships with Actions That Value Others.*

Julia Ballenger is a graduate of the University of Texas at Austin. She is the first E. J. Campbell Distinguished Professor in the Department of Secondary Education and Educational Leadership at Stephen F. Austin State University, Nacogdoches, Texas, where she serves as assistant professor and coordinator of the Department of Educational Leadership. She is a member of the College of Education Advisory Board, College of Education Faculty Senate, and the Advisory Board for the University Center. Dr. Ballenger's research includes micropolitics, principal behavior, access to higher education, and leadership styles of African American women principals. Her civic and community services include president of the Stephen

F. Austin State University's Phi Delta Kappa, vice president for membership of the Nacogdoches American Association of University Women, and
member of the University Professional Women's Club.

Faye Hicks-Townes is associate professor at Stephen F. Austin State
University, where she teaches courses in general education methods and
educational research. She earned a doctorate in educational foundations
at the University of Tennessee, Knoxville. Her research interests are
concerned with the social context of learning, particularly as it relates to
women of color.

Carolyn Carr is an associate professor in the Graduate School of Education at Portland State University in Portland, Oregon. She is currently the
coordinator of the Executive Leadership Program. She received her Ph.D.
from The University of Texas at Austin after a 20-year career as a public
school teacher, counselor, and administrator. Her research has focused on
principal preparation, gender and language issues related to school leadership, and school policy and politics. Dr. Carr recently served as guest
editor of a special series in the *Journal of School Leadership* entitled "Pro-
fessing Educational Leadership: Experiences for the University Classroom." She is also editor of the 2004 yearbook of the National Council of
Professors of Educational Administration.

Betty Alford is associate professor in the Department Chair of Secondary
Education and Educational Leadership at Stephen F. Austin State University in Nacogdoches, Texas. She earned her Ph.D. in educational administration from the University of Texas at Austin. Dr. Alford's professional
experiences include service as a principal, assistant principal, high school
counselor, service center consultant, and teacher. She has served as project director for the Gaining Early Awareness and Readiness for Undergraduate Programs (GEAR UP) project, a $2.8 million U.S. Department
of Education partnership grant, for 5 years and as doctoral program coordinator for 3 years.